AMERICAN HERITAGE

February, 1972 • Volume XXIII, Number 2

© 1972 by American Heritage Publishing Co., Inc. All rights reserved under Berne and Pan-American Copyright Conventions. Reproduction in whole or in part of any article without permission is prohibited.

LETTER FROM THE EDITOR

To most of our readers, Bruce Catton means Civil War. Mention his name and they hear tramping feet, the music of far-off bands, and, of course, that renowned stillness at Appomattox, where the great protagonists played out the last, gentlemanly scene. Somehow Catton makes all this come to such vivid life that it all seems only yesterday, so much so that about ten years ago one young lady in our company, breathlessly admiring but rather lightly instructed in American history, asked us which side Mr. Catton had fought on himself, the Union or the Confederate.

We are privileged to announce now that the old campaigner is out of the trenches, has put away his knapsack full of Pulitzer Prizes and honorary degrees, and is busy with a civilian task. It is tempting to say that, like the postbellum United States, he is Opening Up the West, but the truth compels us to confess that it is really the Old Northwest or, to be specific, Michigan. Catton was born there, at Petoskey, and grew up not far away in a small town called Benzonia, in a family of educators and ministers of the Gospel. He has a place now in the same northwest corner of Michigan's Lower Peninsula, a house in the woods near Frankfort, overlooking not only the lake on our cover but also the vastness of Lake Michigan beyond—a fine vantage point from which to keep an eye on nature, the changing seasons, and the occasional steamboat in the distance. There, away from his office in New York, he has been writing the book that we are beginning to excerpt in this issue. There will be three more installments in the magazine before the entire book, tentatively titled *A Michigan Boyhood*, is published sometime this fall by Doubleday & Company.

Like all of Bruce Catton's work, the title is deceptively simple. The author is an intensely private man, bent not at all on the modern mode of self-revelation. That is, the subject is more Michigan than Catton; he appears in the story, to be sure, but as a sharer of experience and witness to change. And as far as change goes—the changes that stripped the great forests, that uprooted and ruined the Indian, the changes that polluted and destroyed—he is a quietly hostile witness. Looking into the cold North where, he says with only slight exaggeration, there is nothing between Michigan and Siberia but the watchful radar towers and the DEW line, he makes a worried assessment of the future of our society.

Originally, Catton left Michigan in his teens, to join the Navy in World War I, but he was too young and too late for action. After attending Oberlin College for three years, he became a newspaper man in Cleveland, Boston, and finally Washington. Then, during World War II, he was in public relations for the War Production Board, moving on later to Henry Wallace's Department of Commerce; eventually all this experience was distilled into a devastating but, he says wryly, little-read book called *The War Lords of Washington*. His own road to Appomattox, which he had been privately following as a hobby since boyhood, did not open up until he was fifty-one and published his first Civil War book, *Mr. Lincoln's Army*. After three publishers who must still regret it had turned the manuscript down, Doubleday picked it up, and the rest is not only history but very good history—a sizable shelf of it.

That was twenty years ago, and for the last eighteen of them Bruce Catton has also been closely associated with AMERICAN HERITAGE magazine. He was the first editor of our hard-bound series, beginning in December, 1954; in 1959, busy with his career in writing and lecturing, he moved aside to be our Senior Editor, albeit a very active one. To outsiders the thought of so dazzling a career beginning after fifty is no doubt reassuring; to us on the magazine staff it has been a constant delight. And now there is *Michigan*, which, if you will read it carefully, seems to be a kind of parable about our whole country, and the promise and peril of American life a hundred and seven years after Appomattox supposedly solved our problems.

—*Oliver Jensen*

AMERICAN HERITAGE

The Magazine of History

SENIOR EDITOR
Bruce Catton

EDITOR
Oliver Jensen
ARTICLES EDITOR
E. M. Halliday
EXECUTIVE EDITOR
Nat Brandt
ASSOCIATE EDITORS
Barbara Klaw   Bernard A. Weisberger
ART DIRECTOR
Emma Landau
PICTURE EDITORS
Carla Davidson   Mary Dawn Earley
ASSISTANT: Devorah Kanter
COPY EDITOR
Joyce O'Connor

CONSULTING EDITOR: Joan Paterson Kerr
CONTRIBUTING EDITOR: Robert C. Alberts

ADVISORY BOARD
Carl Carmer   Eric F. Goldman
Gerald Carson   Louis C. Jones
Henry Steele Commager   Alvin M. Josephy, Jr.
Marshall B. Davidson   Howard H. Peckham
John A. Garraty   Francis S. Ronalds
S. K. Stevens

AMERICAN HERITAGE PUBLISHING CO., INC.
PRESIDENT AND PUBLISHER
Paul Gottlieb
EDITOR IN CHIEF
Joseph J. Thorndike
SENIOR EDITOR
Richard M. Ketchum
EDITORIAL ART DIRECTOR
Murray Belsky

AMERICAN HERITAGE is published every two months by American Heritage Publishing Co., Inc.; editorial and executive offices, 551 Fifth Avenue, New York, N.Y. 10017. Treasurer, Marjorie C. Dyer; Secretary, John C. Taylor III. Correspondence about subscriptions should be sent to American Heritage Subscription Office, 383 West Center Street, Marion, Ohio 43302. Single copies: $5.00. Annual subscriptions: $20.00 in U.S. and Canada; $21.00 elsewhere.

A ten-year Index covering Volumes VI–XV is available at $5.00, and a five-year Index of Volumes XVI–XX at $3.50.

AMERICAN HERITAGE will consider but assumes no responsibility for unsolicited materials. Title registered U.S. Patent Office. Second-class postage paid at New York, N.Y., and at additional mailing offices.

Sponsored by
American Association for State & Local History · Society of American Historians

CONTENTS *February, 1972 · Volume XXIII, Number 2*

A MICHIGAN BOYHOOD *by Bruce Catton*	4
THE SIEGE OF QUEBEC, 1775–1776 *by Michael Pearson*	8
THE DROUGHT AND THE DOLE *by Robert Cowley*	16
THE CARPENTER-ARCHITECTS OF KEY WEST *by Roger Starr*	20
THE GOOD PROVIDER *by Robert C. Alberts*	26
THE SQUARE DANCING MASTER *by David L. Lewis*	48
THE SPIES WHO WENT OUT IN THE COLD *by Neil R. Stout*	52
ROSA PARKS WOULDN'T BUDGE *by Janet Stevenson*	56
THE WPA'S AMAZING ARTISTIC RECORD OF AMERICAN DESIGN *by Marshall B. Davidson*	65
POSTSCRIPTS TO HISTORY	109
THE REVISIONIST: THE CHERRY-TREE CAPER *Drawn by Michael Ramus*	112

COVER: Bruce Catton, our noted fellow editor and colleague, loves his native Michigan and spends as much time there as he can. This picture of him, wearing a characteristic old felt hat, was taken near his summer home in the northwestern part of the Lower Peninsula by Daniel Kramer. It was a misty autumn morning beside Crystal Lake; from his hideaway in the woods above it he could look out at Lake Michigan beyond, and Sleeping Bear Dune and other features of the rugged land he describes so eloquently in the memoir beginning on the next page. As for the back cover, we all subscribe wholeheartedly to the noble sentiment in this charming old wood engraving, originally the frontispiece of a book on "Female Education" by Erasmus Darwin, the poet-scientist grandfather of Charles Darwin. Furnished us by the Yale University Library, it comes from the Philadelphia edition, published in 1798, and ought to hang in front of every television set.

FIRST OF FOUR INSTALLMENTS

A FAMOUS HISTORIAN RECALLS THE COUNTRY WHERE HE GREW UP

A Michigan Boyhood

By BRUCE CATTON

COPYRIGHT © 1972 BY BRUCE CATTON

First there was the ice; two miles high, hundreds of miles wide, and many centuries deep. It came down from the darkness at the top of the world, and it hung down over the eaves, and our Michigan country lay along the line of the overhang. To be sure, all of the ice was now gone. It had melted, they said, ten thousand years ago; but they also pointed out that ten thousand years amounted to no more than a flick of the second hand on the geologic time clock. It was recent; this was the frontier, where you could stand in the present and look out into the past, and when you looked you now and then got an eerie sense that the world had not yet been completed. What had been might be again. There was a hint, at times, when the dead-winter wind blew at midnight, that the age of ice might someday return, sliding down the country like a felt eraser over a grade-school blackboard, rubbing out all of the sums and sentences that had been so carefully written down; leaving, barely legible, a mocking *quod erat demonstrandum*.

Now and then it was a little confusing. The contrast between the old and the new was too great. There was nothing for the mind to get hold of; what probably had been was hardly more real than what possibly might yet be. We lived less than three hundred miles from Detroit, which seemed to be a door looking into the future, showing unimaginable things; and three hundred miles in the other direction, off into the desolate north country, lay the bleak spine of the upper peninsula of Michigan, a reef of the oldest rocks on earth—Precambrian rocks laid down before there were any living creatures to be fossilized, rocks dead since the hour of creation. There was no way to comprehend that reef. The geologists said that it was two billion years old, or perhaps three billion—a measure of the age of the earth—and there is no way to digest any such figures. The mind cannot grasp a time span like that. The scientist's book is as far beyond our comprehension as the book of Genesis, which simply asserts that the entire job was done in six days, with a seventh day for rest. Take it either way you please, you wind up with something you have to accept on faith.

In any case, the north country is very old. It is also very empty. Take a two-hundred-mile tape measure, long enough to span the lower peninsula of Michigan from east to west, and move it northward, broadside on; once you pass Lake Superior your tape strikes nothing at all except primitive wilderness, clusters of stubby firs, tamarack bogs, and barren tundra, with the leftover fragments of the old age of ice lying beyond. Take the tape on to the North Pole and go down the far side of the globe; you will be deep in Siberia before you strike anything more than a trading post or a mining camp or an outpost of national defense.

It was and is all empty, a land that could not be lived in except by a few undemanding Stone Age tribes, and across its emptiness lies the gray shadow of a profound unease. The ice age, if it comes back, will come from up here. And if that, after all, is a thin chance, a crippling wisdom has reached us in this century: The Enemy may some day come down from the north, aiming at Detroit and Chicago and everything they stand

Opposite: A glimpse of Michigan as it was a hundred years ago, preserved today at Hartwick Pines State Park

PHOTOGRAPHED FOR AMERICAN HERITAGE BY DANIEL KRAMER

for, including ourselves, bringing fire instead of cold. That is why I can look out of the window in the room where I write and see unobtrusive white domes on the skyline—radar domes scanning the north country with unsleeping attention. To be sure, we do not give them a great deal of thought. Life in Michigan north of the industrial zone is easy and pleasant, with fish to be caught and clear lakes for swimming, lonely streams for canoes and the big lake itself for larger craft; here it is possible to escape from the steamy, overcrowded, overactive Middle West and get back to something we knew long ago, when it was good enough just to breathe the clean air and feel sunlight and wind on your shoulders. But the white domes are there, and it is not quite possible to forget what they stand for. This is the frontier, a place for looking before and after, where we try to think what we shall do with the future, only to discover that we are conditioned by what we have already done with the past. The frontier! Three quarters of a century have passed since we announced that America's last frontier was gone forever. We were wrong. In spite of ourselves we have moved on into an undiscovered world. We shall always have a frontier, because we are not facing a finite North American continent whose menaces and surprises must someday all be tabulated; we are facing an infinite universe, and the last challenge has yet to be formulated. Possibly we shall encounter it tomorrow morning.

It may be that the Indians knew something.

One of the odd things about this Michigan frontier is that it contained a people who may have been the first metal users on earth; or if not the first, among the first, isolated here thousands of miles from anything that would later be described as civilization. In the land on and near the base of the Keweenaw Peninsula, which juts out into the cold surf along the southern shore of Lake Superior, there lived a people who made things out of copper—axes, chisels, knives, spear points, ornaments of all kinds. They started doing this possibly seven thousand years ago—an immensely long time as human history is measured: before Abraham tended his flocks near Ur of the Chaldees, indeed before Ur so much as existed—and doing it they stood at the very threshold of technological development.

It was fairly simple. They were primitive forest people who had stumbled into an area where there were lumps of pure copper waiting to be picked up and used—not copper ore but virgin copper, in shining big nuggets. To them a lump of copper was no doubt just another stone with pleasing characteristics. It could be hammered and ground into shape with less effort, and to far better effect, than the bits of taconite, flint, quartzite, and slate they had been using, and the tools and weapons made of it were far more effective than the stone implements they already had. As they went on using it, they began to learn things about copper. They found that most of it was embedded in hard quartz, and sooner or later they learned how to extract these lumps of pure metal so that they could take them home and make things out of them. (Dig away the earth and expose the ledge that contains these copper nuggets; build a hot fire on it, then pour cold water on the heated rock so that it cracks. Once it cracks, the copper can be gouged out with wooden spuds and stone hammers.) They also learned how to treat the copper so that it would not become brittle under all the hammering and grinding—heat it, plunge it in water, work on it some more, repeat the heat-and-water treatment; these Indians had evolved what metallurgists would later call annealing.

While they did all of this, the earth beneath their feet was still taking shape. The level of what would be known as the Great Lakes (still fresh from the glaciers in those days) rose and fell in centuries-long rhythm. Some of the copper-culture sites went two hundred feet under water, then emerged long after with their charred fire pits and abandoned stone hammers to draw the attention of prospectors, land lookers, and scientists. The land itself rose, ten feet or more in the course of a century, for generation after generation; there is a theory that the resilient earth was slowly springing back into shape once the overwhelming weight of the ice sheet was removed. As the earth rose, it cut off the old outlet of the Great Lakes at North Bay in Ontario. Now the current of the lakes moved down through Lake Erie and broke away across the Niagara escarpment. And while all of these changes were taking place, the Indians who made things out of copper continued to ply their trade. They had copper mines and coppersmiths and some sort of export trade in the finished product at a time when all the rest of the New World and most of the Old lived deep in the age of chipped flint and polished stone. Clearly, these people were right on the edge of entering the age of metals.

It was no great distance away from them. To the extraction of pure metal from conglomerate ores was only one more step; from smelting to casting was only one step beyond that; these steps taken, the Indians would have been well on their way, and what they could do with one metal could presently have been done with another. (Bear in mind that these people were living squarely on top of one of the richest deposits of iron ore on earth.) They had the mental capacity to figure out and to take these steps. No one who has examined the mathematics, the astronomy, and the intricate, labyrinthine structures of abstract thought that came later in Central America and Mexico can doubt that the American red man was qualified for any sort of advance he might care to make.

The trouble with that kind of advance is that there is

no end to it. Development becomes compulsive. Once you take the first step you have committed yourself to take the last, someday, even if the last step goes straight off the edge of a precipice. The age of applied technology has one terrible aspect—each new technique has to be exploited to its absolute limit, until man becomes the victim of his own skills. The conquest of nature cannot end in a negotiated peace. Invent a simple device like the automobile to get you from here to there more quickly than you could go without it; before long you are in bondage to it, so that you build your cities and shape your countryside and reorder your entire life in the light of what will be good for the machine instead of what will be good for you. Detroit has shown us how that works.

Yet somehow these copper-country Indians never took that next step. With one foot on the threshold they paused, then turned away, guided by simple inertia or by an uncanny prescience, whichever you prefer. The use of copper declined, then finally ceased altogether, as the bits of virgin metal became harder to find. The Indians made certain inventions—birch-bark canoes, frail craft indeed for the stormy lakes, but so well conceived that when the white man arrived he went on using them for centuries and still duplicates the flawless pattern in aluminum; and snowshoes, ingenious devices of rawhide thongs strung on frames of birch and ash, enabling men to travel across country in the drifted wintertime. But with things like these the Indians stopped. They remained in the Stone Age, with its simplicities, its limited horizons, and its strange, chilling mythology, which lay between an uneasy belief in magic and a groping faith (half dark suspicion and half desperate hope) that there are unseen powers all about, to be fled from or to be appealed to depending on the whim of the moment. They took the world as they found it. In the north country they remained hunters and fishermen, now and then trading furs for corn with the tribes farther south; in the lower peninsula, where soil and climate were just a little more favorable, they took to part-time farming, and in winter the men went off on hunting expeditions, and in the spring they tapped the maple trees and made sugar. Life went on without very much change, and the pines and the hardwood forests lay across the lake country like a great cool twilight, lived in but not exactly used.

Then at last the men who could use this country began to appear: Frenchmen, who filtered in here about the time when the English were looking at Virginia and Massachusetts. They hoisted the fleur de lys on the ground overlooking the rapids of the St. Marys River, while the Sun King was advancing his realm toward bankruptcy by building the ruinous palace at Versailles, and they ventured along the shingle and sand of the endless beaches and into the shallow inlets that opened the way into the unknown back country. They were eternally inquisitive, looking for furs to ornament robes and make hats for courtiers, for waterways leading to China (they thought briefly they had found one when they got to Green Bay on the western side of Lake Michigan; then they thought it lay beyond the next height of land), and as a matter of fact they were looking for something they could not have defined, because this new world promised more than it had yet delivered.

The first of them apparently was a man known as Etienne Brulé, a lieutenant of Samuel de Champlain, and he got up to the Straits of Mackinac and the St. Marys River country before any European ever stepped on Plymouth Rock. He was looking for furs, for new country, for experiences he could not have had in Europe; he found what he sought, he paid for it, and probably it was all worth it. He lived with the Indians in nameless wigwam-towns along Lake Superior, and sometimes he got on well with his hosts and sometimes he waged a one-man war against them. No one is quite sure just what became of him; the legend is that he was killed in some campfire row, and that the Indians who killed him admired his daring so much that they cut out his heart and ate it, hoping to acquire some of his virtues. His story flickers out inconclusively, somewhere between the forest and the biggest of the lakes, and if he was the first European to lose himself and to die of it in the great north country, he was far from being the last. One of the things the New World offered to the questing European was a chance to go off into nowhere and disappear.

At times it seems as if the country itself resisted the European invasion more effectively than the Indians did, although the Indians were far from passive. Men disappeared in the long forests, and all anyone ever knew about them was that they were gone forever. There was Father René Menard, for instance, a priest who established a mission on Keweenaw Bay in the year 1660; he set out one winter's day on a trip into the trackless interior, and that was the last of him, and whether he was killed by suspicious savages or simply by winter starvation is not known. There was also the ship *Griffin*, built a few years after Father Menard's disappearance by the great French explorer La Salle, who put together and launched a stout little square-rigger and sailed all the way to Green Bay. He loaded her with furs, enough to finance an ambitious venture into the Mississippi country if he could just get the cargo back to Montreal, and sent her off toward the lower lakes. The *Griffin* never made it, and to this day no one knows what happened to her except that she sailed off into the storms and slipped over the edge of the world—first in a long succession of ships to be lost with all hands on the Great Lakes.

CONTINUED ON PAGE 81

A COLONY PRESERVED

THE SIEGE OF QUEBEC, 1775-1776

By MICHAEL PEARSON

The key to control of Canada was a city whose defenders doubted they could hold out for long once the American Rebels attacked

Sixteen years after General James Wolfe's famous assault on Quebec, the city was subjected to another siege—and another storming—that, though less celebrated, was vitally important to Americans in the early months of their revolution.

It was a dramatic episode in Revolutionary history that is exceptionally well documented. This article, based mainly on firsthand accounts by participants, has been adapted by Michael Pearson, an English author, from his new book about the Revolution, Those Damned Rebels, to be published this winter by G. P. Putnam's Sons.

The perspective may seem strange to some readers, since, as the title of the book suggests, the action is seen not from the American viewpoint but through the eyes of the British, who, in Canada in the winter of 1775, were in a situation that appeared very grave indeed.

On New Year's Eve it began to snow again. The wind blew up suddenly from the northeast and howled cold across the icy wastes of northern Canada.

That night, on Quebec's high, thick stone walls, the sentries—mainly civilians unused to the rigors of guard duty—huddled against the battlements for protection against the blizzard and eyed the lights they

THE TWO OPPONENTS: *opposite, Sir Guy Carleton, an undated portrait by an unknown artist; right, General Richard Montgomery pointing to a map of the city where he would fall, silhouetted from an 1858 engraving by Alonzo Chappel. The Carleton portrait is used by permission of the Earl and Countess of Malmesbury.*

Hugging the waterside, in this water color painted about 1777 by James Hunter, is the Lower Town of Quebec, focus of the main American attack. Atop the cliff, in the Upper Town, is the Citadel, flying the British flag.

In a giant pincers move, American Generals Richard Montgomery and Benedict Arnold converged on Quebec in late 1775. On the old (1807) base map at right we trace in bold type the movements of their armies. Arnold arrived first outside the gates of the city after an arduous trek through Maine. Montgomery joined him after capturing St. Johns, Chambly (spelt "Chamblis" and just above St. Johns), and Montreal. Below, British governor Sir Guy Carleton is shown reviewing the small garrison in the Place d'Armes at Montreal prior to Montgomery's seizure of the city.

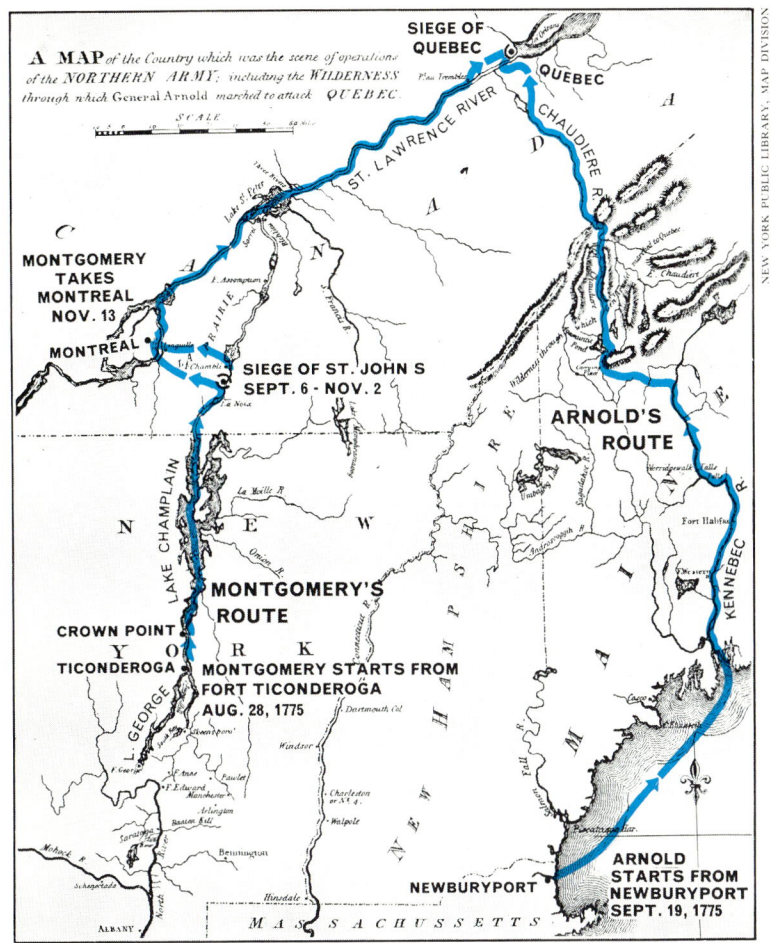

could see moving in the darkness: the lanterns of the besieging Rebels who encircled the upper part of the town.

The storming of the city was imminent. For three weeks the garrison had waited, tensed for attack under constant shelling. Every day reports had come in of the Rebels' preparations—of the scaling ladders they had made, of the weather conditions that General Montgomery favored, of the assault points he had selected, of the reinforcements joining him.

In that grim December of 1775 the city of Quebec was the last small portion of Canada that the British still controlled. Early in September, some three months after the Battle of Bunker Hill, an invading army of nearly two thousand American Rebels, led by General Richard Montgomery—who had taken over command at the last minute from the ill Philip Schuyler—advanced up Lake Champlain across the Canadian border. St. Johns and Chambly—the two main towns on the Richelieu River that connected the lake to the St. Lawrence—were soon under siege, and by October advance Rebel units were threatening Montreal.

On the morning of September 7 the news of the Rebel strike across the border reached the Château St. Louis in Quebec. From this majestic gray stone building with its round slate-roofed towers the British had ruled Canada for the sixteen years since they had wrested the province from the French.

Immediately, Sir Guy Carleton, Canada's aggressive, buoyant governor, hurried to Montreal to organize what forward defense he could. In Quebec he left the lieutenant governor, Hector Cramahé—a rather anxious civil servant with little knowledge of military techniques—with orders to prepare the city for siege.

By then Carleton knew that the only hope the British had of retain-

THE PUBLIC ARCHIVES OF CANADA

11

ANNE S. K. BROWN MILITARY COLLECTION, BROWN UNIVERSITY, PROVIDENCE, R.I.

ing even a toehold in Canada lay in Quebec, which—built as it was on the side of a cliff at the protective junction of the St. Lawrence and St. Charles rivers—was brilliantly sited for defense. But the Governor, though normally optimistic by temperament, was gloomy about his chances of holding even that fortress city. "I think our fate extremely doubtful, to say nothing worse," he was to write to London in November.

The British were still absorbing the first impact of the revolt. The armies that would be crossing the Atlantic in a few months' time were still a subject of discussion in Whitehall. To protect the whole vastness of Canada, as reports of Rebel preparations streamed into Quebec that summer, Carleton had barely six hundred troops.

Certainly, there was little hope of reinforcement. All the way down the Atlantic coast, the royal governors had either sought refuge on British warships or were under arrest or, in one case, had joined the Rebels. There were troops in Boston—then an island connected to the mainland by a narrow isthmus—but they were threatened and outnumbered by the newly formed Continental Army that blocked all the land approaches to the town.

Carleton sent an urgent request for help to Boston, but he did not expect much in the way of practical response. In London, from 3,500 miles away, the problem of manpower in the province seemed relatively simple. The Earl of Dartmouth, secretary of state for the colonies, had ordered Carleton to raise a force of two thousand Canadians; then, after mature reflection by the Cabinet, the figure was increased to three thousand. He even dispatched the equipment for them. But Whitehall was still living in a world of fantasy. The Canadians had declined to send delegates to the congress of Rebels in Philadelphia—who indiscreetly had expressed anti-Catholic sentiments in an appeal to the king—but they were not keen to fight them. Carleton's recruitment drive was a failure. In fact, as he protested angrily, more Canadians joined the Rebels than enrolled in the service of the king—mostly Protestants, who were resentful because the Quebec Act had just brought recognition to the Catholic Church in the province but who were Canadians for all that.

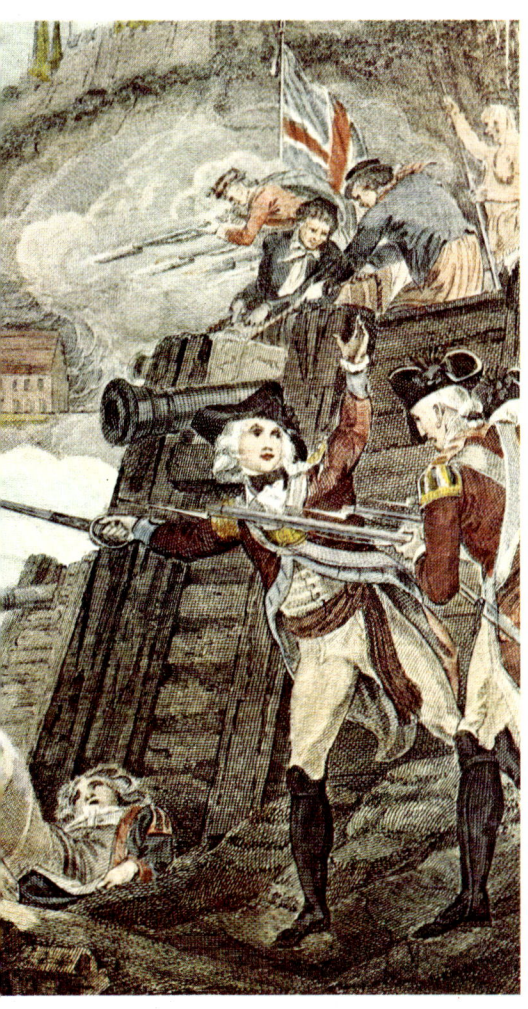

The engraving at left, a romanticized depiction of Montgomery's death, was done in 1789 and errs in its details. The General, mortally wounded but still standing next to the American flag, clasps his chest in pain, while American troops climb toward the heights of Quebec. At his feet are two dying aides-de-camp, thought to be Captains Jacob Cheesman and John McPherson. The engraving below, probably contemporary, shows Montgomery's body being borne through the streets of the city before burial with full military honors, a gracious gesture on the part of Carleton.

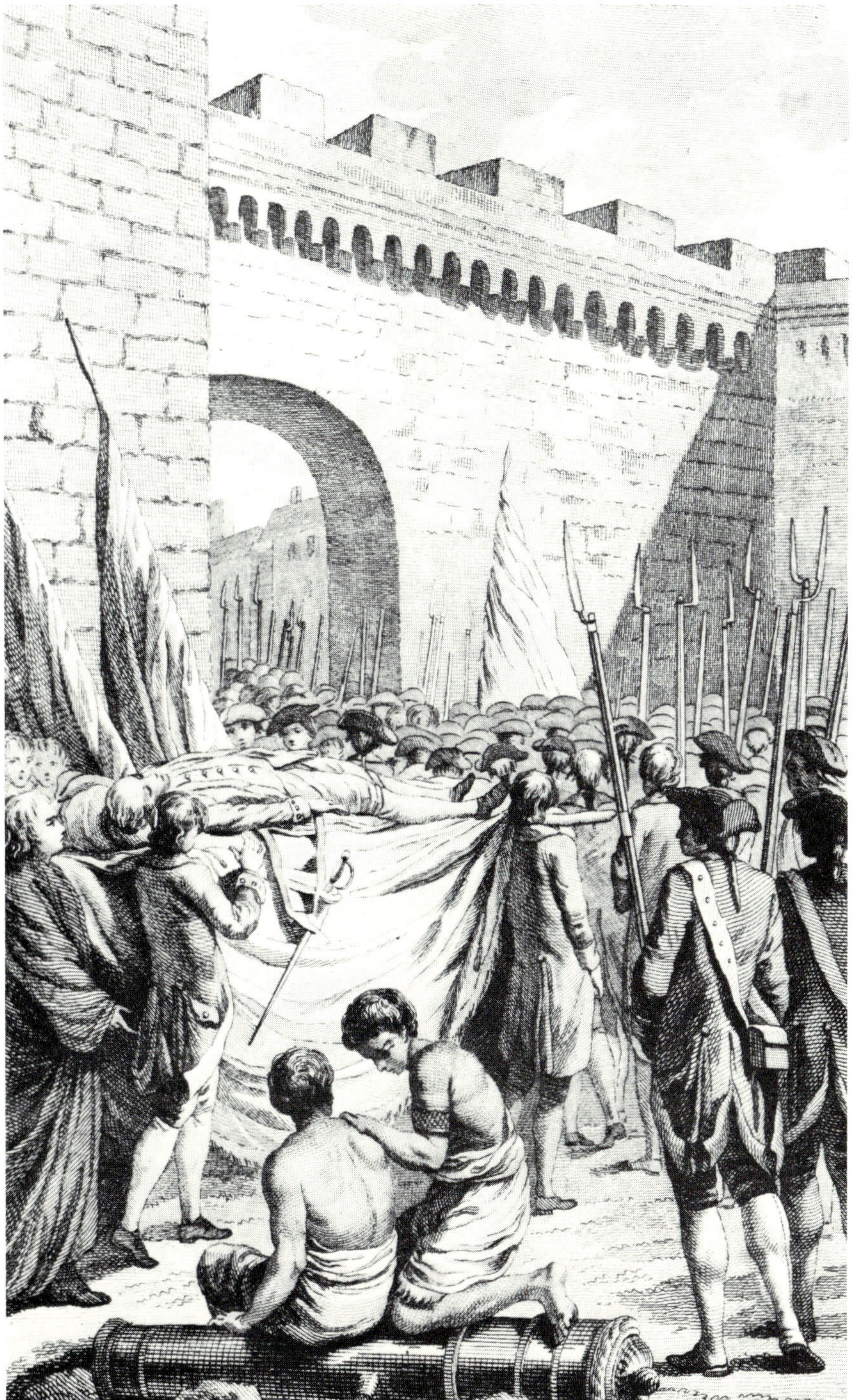

PRINTS DIVISION, METROPOLITAN MUSEUM OF ART

Unhappily, the Governor awaited the inevitable, although he did what little he could to postpone it. On October 19 Chambly was captured by the Rebels, and on November 2 St. Johns fell. There was nothing now to divert them from Montreal.

In Quebec, meanwhile, Cramahé was supervising the final preparations for the defense of the city. The high walls that reached round the upper part of the town between the two rivers had been repaired. Civilians were being trained to use the big guns on the ramparts that covered the approaches to the city over the wide plateau, the Plains of Abraham. Four merchant ships had been fitted out with cannon.

Threatened as it soon would be by Montgomery's troops, Quebec was not in an enviable situation. But on

November 3 the city's prospects grew dramatically and unbelievably worse. News reached the Château St. Louis of an enormous danger from an entirely unexpected direction. A letter addressed to John Manir—an incorrect spelling, it was assumed rightly, for a Quebec merchant with Rebel sympathies named John Mercier—was seized from an Indian courier. It was from Benedict Arnold, who claimed that he was at Dead River with a force of "2,000 men . . . to restore liberty to our brethren of Canada"—an exaggeration; the force was closer to 750 Americans.

Dead River was south of Quebec in the vast rugged wilderness of Maine that, in November when the territory was snowbound, the British regarded as impassable. Although Arnold was magnifying his numbers, Cramahé and his advisers, as they considered his startling letter, had no way of knowing that.

As the British must have realized when they studied the maps, if Arnold truly had brought a force to Dead River, it meant that he had travelled with boats and baggage by an old Indian route leading from the Atlantic up the rapids-choked Kennebec River. This effort involved hauling their equipment over portages—one of twelve miles. To reach Quebec it would mean traversing Lake Megantic and the Chaudière River. In winter, for a force of men who were not all woodsmen, it was unbelievable.

However, Cramahé's initial incredulity was soon dispelled. On November 9, just six days after the arrival of Arnold's letter in Quebec, the Rebels were sighted from the city at Point Levis just across the water. But they could not attempt a crossing in the canoes of the Indians who had joined them, for a gale was soon churning the broad river.

Although the weather checked Arnold, the St. Lawrence was not too rough for a flotilla of bigger boats under the command of Colonel Allan Maclean, who was returning to Quebec with the remnants of a small force that had failed abysmally in an attempt to relieve St. Johns. Maclean, who had raised a corps of loyalist emigrant Scots, was a professional soldier, and it was with some relief that Cramahé handed over to him the military command of the city.

On November 13 the gale blew itself out. That night, despite the British ships and the small craft that patrolled between them, Arnold and his men slipped across the river, landed at Wolfe's Cove, and climbed the same cliffs—now made easier with a path—that the British had clambered up to reach the Plains of Abraham in the celebrated assault sixteen years earlier. By the time one of the British patrol boats detected them, they had almost completed landing on the north shore. As the boat approached to investigate, the Rebels opened fire, and the craft veered sharply to carry the alarm to the *Lizard*, the frigate anchored off the town.

That morning the Rebels marched to within eight hundred yards of the city and gave three great cheers. The men watching them from the guns at the walls put their matches to the touchholes of the twenty-four-pounders, which were loaded with grape and canister shot. The guns flashed, the explosions following each other loudly in quick, uneven succession. For a few seconds smoke obscured the view from the ramparts. Then, as it cleared, the artillerymen saw that the Rebels were dropping back.

Later in the day Arnold sent a letter to the town under a flag of truce, demanding surrender "in the name of the united colonies." "If I am obliged to carry the town by storm," he warned, "you may expect every severity practised on such occasions and the merchants who may now save their property will probably be involved in the general ruin."

During those critical hours, as they waited for Arnold to attack, the situation of the city seemed very grave. All too soon thick sea ice would block the approach to the St. Lawrence, and no ships from England would be able to reach the town until the spring. Arnold, however, would soon be strongly supported. With Montreal on the point of surrender, it would not be long before Montgomery's army advanced with its guns down the river to join the besiegers.

Cramahé summoned a council of war in the Château St. Louis to decide policy; present were Maclean, the captains of the naval ships, the masters of some of the cargo vessels, the colonels of the militia, and the town mayor. The anxious men in the big room in the gloomy château must have been only too conscious that sixteen years earlier, the French Field Marshal Louis de Montcalm had presided over a similar conference. Then it had been the British who were outside the walls.

The French, however, had been in Quebec in some strength. Montcalm had had regular soldiers to defend the town. Now, Maclean had only a handful of trained men—thirty-five marines, one or two gunners, and a few fusiliers. In addition, he had his Royal Highland Emigrants, whom he had recruited in Nova Scotia and Newfoundland in the summer; but they had only been under arms a few weeks.

The truth was that if Quebec was to be held, the main brunt would fall on civilians—merchants, civil servants, sailors, and fishermen. The town's walls were long, and though the civilians had guns to fight off attack, they had very few experienced gunners.

On the other hand Quebec was a fortress that had never been taken by storm. Moncalm's fatal error had been to march out from behind his strong protection and fight the British in straight combat. Furthermore, there was enough food in the city to last until spring, and adequate ammunition—if only the amateur garrison could succeed in firing it. The war council decided to fight, to hold Quebec to "the last extremity."

There was still just time for a ship to get through to the Atlantic before the ice closed in. A naval officer, it itself, were still in British hands.

For four days after they paraded in front of the walls on the Plains of Abraham, Arnold's men, quartered in nearby houses, besieged the town. Then, on the eighteenth, the men on duty on the walls saw the enemy trailing west across the snow in a long and ragged column. Reports row, rocky streams, the Americans had set up batteries of guns.

By then, Montreal—and more—was in Rebel hands. As soon as St. Johns had fallen, Carleton had known that he could not even mount a temporary defense of the city because of the lukewarm attitude of its residents. "It is obvious that as soon

With the Surprise *and* Isis *in the van, a British relief squadron broke through the winter ice on the St. Lawrence River and reached Quebec on May 6, 1776, thus effectively lifting the siege of the strategic city. This water color was done by either British artist Charles Turner Warren or his son Alfred William Warren.*

was decided, would be sent to Britain to describe the exact situation. Pilots would go with him to bring in the relief forces on the off chance—which seemed remote at the moment—that the garrison could hold out until the ice melted. A secret signal—a blue pendant over a Union Jack and the firing of five guns—would inform an approaching fleet that the ships which remained, and the city came in that they had withdrawn to Pointe aux Trembles, twenty miles up the St. Lawrence, to wait for Montgomery.

By the morning of November 19, there was still no news in Quebec of Carleton or Montreal, but reports had arrived of Rebel plans to stop his withdrawal downriver. At Sorel, where the Berthier Islands split the waters of the St. Lawrence into nar- as the Rebels appear outside the town in force," he had written to London, "the townspeople will give it up on the best terms they can procure. I shall try to retire the evil hour . . . though all my hopes of succour now begin to vanish."

On the eleventh—eight days before Cramahé held his crisis council of war in the Château St. Louis—Carleton had been warned that the

CONTINUED ON PAGE 104

15

HERBERT HOOVER'S
DISMAL DILEMMA

The Drought and the Dole

By ROBERT COWLEY

Few places are more unpleasant than Washington in the summer, and the summer of 1930 was worse than most. The pressures of the business downturn had kept Herbert Hoover a prisoner in the White House through a hot June and a hotter July —the stock-market crash was less than a year old—and in those days before air conditioning, editorial writers were beginning to express concern for the President's health.

Whenever he could break away for a weekend, Hoover would lead a caravan of Cabinet members and other influential guests to his Rapidan River fishing camp three hours away in the Virginia mountains; even there the heat was inescapable that summer. He had announced plans for an August vacation in the Rockies, where he proposed to make a leisurely tour of the national parks, and his most ardent critics could not deny

COPYRIGHT © 1972 BY ROBERT COWLEY

that he certainly had earned the rest.

"The President, it is understood, has more than an interest in nature and a love of the outdoors in visiting the Western region," the *New York Times* commented. "Some of his friends assert that he desires to test the strength of his own position after fourteen months in office. . . ." The events of recent months had certainly tarnished his position, but as yet there was little indication that the damage was much more than the surface wind-erosion of politics. Hoover was an authentic American hero, the managerial genius who had organized relief for starving Belgium and Russia, who had taken command of the broken levees and the submerged fields of the Mississippi River delta during the great flood of 1927. Most people believed him now when he said that the slump had touched bottom—and public trust, like confidence in Insull utilities or the Bank of the United States, could prove the margin of recovery.

The mood of the boom persisted as that steamy summer began. Unemployment, the administration reassured the country, wasn't as bad as the bread lines made it seem. Stocks were drifting downward after an impressive recovery in the spring, but Wall Street blamed that on the doldrums of the season. Not even in

Withered and broken stalks, an abandoned house, and the deeply furrowed, arid land in this vast empty landscape are all that remain of a farm family's life and livelihood. The defeated people have long since gone away. The photograph was taken by Dorothea Lange in 1938.

LIBRARY OF CONGRESS

The cheerful giver, 1930

Grinning cheerful giver, 1931

Glum cheerful giver and wife, 1932

the best years of the Jazz Age had so many Americans travelled in Europe, and those who didn't get over still had enough money to spend a half million dollars a day emulating Bobby Jones's grand slam on miniature-golf-course putting greens. They fretted about the heat as much as the Depression. If clouds remained on the Presidential horizon, few, unfortunately, were rain clouds.

It was hot—hotter than anyone could remember. The country had never known a month as hot as July, the weather bureau said. In Arkansas during one forty-three-day stretch, the mercury reached 100 degrees or more on all but one day. A grocer in Petersburg, Indiana, opened up his store one morning to find a newly hatched chick hopping on top of a basket of eggs; the heat had been as effective as a sitting hen. A newspaper report from Quitman, Georgia, stated more or less seriously that a small field of popcorn popped spontaneously on the stalk. The story was straight out of Paul Bunyan, of course; so were the heat and the drought. For it was dry, too. Descendants of a Mrs. Roof in Ohio stirred around in their attic and discovered her diary, which seemed to indicate that only the 1830's had been drier. A great swath of the middle states of America, running from the Chesapeake Bay to the Rocky Mountains, was affected by drought; the prospect not only of crop failure but of water famine threatened perhaps a million farm families in the twenty-seven-state area.

In places the leaves were turn-

Private charity was Mr. Hoover's preferred solution to the vast problems of drought and depression. He wanted the privately supported Red Cross to feed those who were hungry. Before White House press photographers, the President year after year led the way, publicly receiving the Red Cross emblem from the organization's chairman, John Barton Payne.

ing brown in early August; people walked dry-shod in what were ordinarily the river bottoms of the Ohio and the Mississippi, and fish were stranded and were dying in stagnant pools that had lately been trout streams. Water sold for a dollar a barrel in parts of southern Illinois, and motorists were known to have paid as much to have their radiators filled as they did for gas. A southern Ohio farmer named James Mead described how he "chopped down bushes and small trees in order to let the cattle eat the green leaves and thus to keep them from starving while we hoped and prayed for rain. Many birds are dying for lack of food. The seeds of weeds even have failed to ripen. Apples have literally been cooked on the trees. We are hauling water three miles."

A heavy stillness enveloped the land; as day after day passed without rain, the sky took on an eerie copper tinge. Farmers watched helplessly as one crop after another failed that summer. Some went deeper into debt than they were already; others found that not even their vegetable gardens would grow, and lived on root crops and fried green apples. One Arkansas county agent reported that half of his two thousand farm families were without "feed for their stock or food for themselves." His state was the hardest hit; banks were failing along with the crops, and cases of typhoid and pellagra were reported on the increase—the one caused by bad water and the other by vitamin deficiency.

Mark Sullivan, a journalist with close ties to the White House, wrote later that the President turned to the drought "with something like a sense of relief, almost of pleasure." This was the sort of problem he understood: "The drought was concrete; he could get his hands upon it—unlike the intangible forces of depression which in many respects were psychological and came stealthily out of the air." On the morning of Monday, August 11, Hoover returned from his Rapidan camp to learn that the July corn crop was 690,000,000 bushels under the average for the month: the harvest had not been so low in more than a quarter of a century. Red Cross reports made public that day also indicated that people were "actually suffering." On Tuesday the President announced that because of the emergency he was cancelling his trip to the West. All through the following day governors from the drought states debarked at Union Station, and on Thursday the fourteenth, amid a hush of expectancy and a gentle flutter of press releases, they met at the White House to discuss what might be done in the way of immediate relief.

It was a moment that called for a dramatic and open-handed gesture calculated to capture the attention and enlist the sympathy of the whole nation: a special session of Congress or a tour of the scene, a promise of food or money or the initiation of a vast disaster-relief campaign under the auspices of the Red Cross. A little Wilsonian rhetoric—just a little—would have helped. But the theatrical action was not Hoover's style; his performances were always to the front rows only. How many similar opportunities would present themselves in the next two and a half years, and how many would be passed up—turning points that didn't turn?

Herbert Hoover was a humane man in a trap of his own making. Earlier in the year he had cut taxes at the request of business leaders, and now he worried about strains in the budget, which was beginning to show an unaccustomed deficit. The conventional, pre-Keynesian economics of the period viewed an unbalanced budget as a cause of, and not a remedy for, depression; and Hoover, who was hardly a radical in these matters, feared the effect of a sudden outpouring of federal funds, even in the form of loans. Any large-scale federal program, moreover, brought up the touchy question of direct relief. Direct relief from the government, anything that smacked of the notorious British dole, was counter to the principles of American individualism, which the President so strenuously invoked. He maintained that state and local authorities, cooperating with private charity, could handle the problem. "The drought," Sullivan wrote, in setting forth Hoover's position, "lent itself to cure by an American method and in accord with an American tradition that he cherished: i.e., through community generosity and mutual self-help."

Hoover and the governors resolved the dilemma to his ideological satisfaction at least. He persuaded the railroads to haul feed to the afflicted areas at half rates and asked the Red Cross to provide aid for those in the most serious distress; it immediately responded with a pledge of $5,000,000. He exhorted banks and businesses to extend loans to farmers temporarily in need and authorized new road-building projects to give them work. No sooner had the governors departed than the skies of the Midwest burst open. Rain deluged millions of parched acres, and news of the meteorological reprieve inundated Wall Street in a torrent of optimism. Had the Great Engineer turned rainmaker?

The heat spell broke in September, and though the rain clouds disappeared again, the drought receded to the back pages of the newspapers. Unemployment was the big story now, and apple sellers were making their unsettling appearance on street corners, first in New York and soon in all the major cities. Occasionally an item, no less disturbing for its brevity, would recall the late emergency. White farmers in Lonoke County, Arkansas—keep the name in mind—fired into the tents of black laborers imported to work on a state highway. The locals thought they should have the jobs; the National Guard had to be called in to keep peace. Physicians at the Kansas State Fair's Better Babies Contest

CONTINUED ON PAGE 92

At a Red Cross distribution center in Lonoke County, Arkansas, a genial worker deals out food supplies to some grim-faced farm families whose crops have failed in the 1930 drought. Presumably they have all presented the proper applications, properly filled out.

AMERICAN RED CROSS

The Carpenter-Architects of
KEY WEST

By ROGER STARR

Key West, southernmost city in the mainland United States proper, was also in 1880 the largest and most prosperous city in Florida; by 1930, in dizzying contrast, it had become one of the most depressed areas in the United States. It has suffered not only from recurrent overexpectations—perhaps a national affliction—but from recurrent disasters, both human and natural. The wavy ups and downs of Key West's spirits have left their traces on the sand and coral of the small island on which the city stands. On the upswings of its hopes the city produced what few American cities achieve: a distinctive style of architecture. The downswings of its disappointments have permitted its architectural achievement to remain undisturbed; faded, perhaps, but still there. As a result modern Key West is the somewhat startled custodian of a small but priceless architectural treasure.

The city, buoyed now by the surging national demand for fresh shrimp and vacations-cum-outboard-motors, rides the swell of renewed commercial expectations. If these are sounder than their predecessors, prosperity will raise local land values. This trend may well make the sites where the old buildings stand too valuable for the buildings themselves; someone will covet the land as the perfect place for garden apartments or office buildings. The architectural treasure may be in danger. Already there are portents to remind the visitor of similar events in other cities: sudden disappearances of fine buildings, some touches of tarnish where a present owner hopes to sell and believes his site is more attractive than the condition of his house, and, too often, a canny but tasteless substitution on some buildings of architectural rhinestones for architectural diamonds.

Key West's treasure reflects its peculiarly American heritage. Its notable buildings are not public structures, like churches and government buildings, signed with the unmistakable mannerism of an individual architect. The city is notable for domestic structures—the non-palatial homes of the affluent and near-affluent that are ignored in European architectural history but on which many American architects, like Henry H. Richardson, Stanford White, Frank Lloyd Wright, or Philip Johnson, made their original reputations. Key West's domestic buildings are essentially American in still another sense: no professional architect designed them—no one, in fact, designed them at all. They are a spectacular result of carpenter archi-

NEW-YORK HISTORICAL SOCIETY

Naval guns and handsome wooden porches are part of Key West's heritage. Above, a view of Fort Taylor in the 1850's; opposite, an airy stairway of the Otto House built in 1898.

21

Key West's untutored builders wrought in wood with native grace and a somewhat Bahamian flavor. Picture (1) shows a typical house with airy double porches; (2) is a detail of their intricate carving. In (3) the embellished cornice of the Porter House is seen; (4) presents shuttered French doors on the George Carey House, and (5) a sun-splashed decorated gable end of the Curry House. A shutter of the Richard Kemp Moore House is in (6) and a playful balustrade in (7). The details at right show cunning iron- and stonework; (8) and (9) are ornamented gates, the latter on the Vining Harris House; (10) is a vinelike column; (11) doorway grillwork on the La Concha Hotel; (12) and (13) are a sculptured gatepost and gate of the Otto House.

tecture, made by men without formal training who had studied no abstract tables of the strength of the materials and who probably solved the details of design as they built. Their design tables were in their thumbs; their schooling consisted of memories of other buildings, seen in other places, that had accomplished what the carpenters needed. Because they worked in Key West, the carpenter-architects brought with them memories of a number of vessels and seaport homes from their own past. They borrowed what they wanted: widow's walks from New England; roof scuttles for ventilation from ships themselves; long, overhanging eaves and gutters connected to underground cisterns from the West Indies. From these, and from the echoes of fashion that made their way to Key West with its new arrivals over 150 years of history, they derived from time to time a suggestion of contemporary styles: Greek Revival columns and Federal fanlights; later, from the Gothic Revival, gables and window bays; from Creole New Orleans, wrought-iron trellises and balustrades, reproducing these, with tropical fecundity of imagination, in wood.

Wood, of course, constitutes the essential material of the carpenter-architect. This tends to degrade his achievement. Many Europeans cannot overcome their sense that living in a wooden house stigmatizes one as a social and cultural inferior. If taste were more logical, stone and brick houses in Europe might constitute a badge of shame; dwellings there were built in these materials largely because the native hardwood forests had been felled to satisfy other needs: fuel and ships, for example. In forested America, on the other hand, builders were free to use wood generously. Wood was available on Key West, even though little structural-sized timber grows locally. Some came to the city from the salvage of wrecks, the city's first major doomed industry. Some of these wrecks had been

ALL PHOTOGRAPHS BY MICHAEL CARLEBACH AND DAVID KENT

23

Mario Sanchez, a native Key Wester now in his sixties, hand chisels, then paints wood reliefs recalling the town of his boyhood with imagination, gaiety, and delicacy. At top left is the Lowe House, one-time home of a Confederate beauty scornful of the Union soldiery. Below that a Key West black funeral procession swings a brisk good-bye to someone departed. At bottom left and top and center right, are public buildings that do not dwarf the tranquil citizens and horses—the County Court House, the old City Hall, and the old Customs House and Post Office. At bottom, cigar makers pass their working hours listening to a paid reader—a job once held in New York by Samuel Gompers and in Key West by Sanchez's father.

carrying structural-grade lumber from Pensacola and its nearby forests. The cargoes were usually auctioned off in Key West, in part to pay the salvage bill. Lumber was also deliberately imported by Key Westers with the money they made in other transactions—mahogany from Honduras; cypress from the upper Keys, nearer the Florida mainland; pine from the Gulf Coast ports like Pensacola, Mobile, and Pascagoula. Some came in the form of dismantled houses, at least two of which were carried complete but knocked down by their owners, who migrated to Key West from the Bahamas in the 1840's.

Metal nails were in short supply in Key West, however; most of the older houses were assembled mainly without them; mortise and tenon joints held the structural members together. The assembly worked out very well despite the extreme stresses that frequent hurricanes have put on the buildings of Key West. The wooden houses are generally erected on Florida cypress posts, which are sunk into heavy coral or limestone footings. The sills of the houses are pegged to upper ends of the posts. This type of construction is especially hurricane-proof, according to a group of native Key Westers descended from white immigrants from the Bahamas, who call themselves Conchs (rhymes with "tonks," as in "honky-tonks"). They explain that the tree-nailed houses bend in a heavy blow, offering less than rigid resistance to high winds. Whether or not this adequately explains the high survival rate (and the oldest house on the island has withstood every hurricane since 1825), it is a fact that the older homes are built without plaster, which might well crack when the structural frame shifts position. Wooden interior walls, sometimes ornamented with chair rails or base-

CONTINUED ON PAGE 86

THE SANCHEZ ILLUSTRATIONS APPEAR BY COURTESY OF THE SMALL AND FIRST-CLASS KEY WEST GALLERY, EL KIOSKO, OWNED BY MRS. LOUISE WHITE, WHO DISCOVERED THE ARTIST. THE EDITORS WISH TO THANK HER AND MRS. BETTY BRUCE, OF THE MONROE COUNTY PUBLIC LIBRARY, WHO PROVIDED MUCH KNOWLEDGEABLE ASSISTANCE. OWNERS OF SANCHEZ PAINTINGS, COUNTERCLOCKWISE FROM TOP LEFT: DR. & MRS. JERE B. STERN; PRIVATE COLLECTION; MRS. GLORIA K. CONAHAY; MR. & MRS. JAMES E. SHIELDS; MRS. ARDEN CATLIN; MRS. MARGARET PASCHALL.

The Good Provider

"57 VARIETIES" WAS ONLY A SALES SLOGAN, BUT H. J. HEINZ

UNDERSTOOD FROM THE START THAT THERE WAS NO SUBSTITUTE

FOR HONEST PRODUCTS AND WELL-TREATED WORKERS

By ROBERT C. ALBERTS

Pittsburgh, God knows, was no fourth-century Athens, but around 1900 it did have a remarkable group of industrial leaders. The Pittsburgh barons exercised their power and made their fortunes in coal and coke, iron and steel, aluminum and oil, glass, rails, and heavy machinery. Five of them were commanding figures in their time and are legends in ours: Carnegie, Frick, Westinghouse, Mellon, and Heinz. Allan Nevins has called such men the architects of our material progress. They have been called other things as well, all except H. J. Heinz.

Henry John Heinz chose in this most unlikely location—a city built among hills and based on the heaviest of heavy industry—to work at the primary business of feeding people. For fifty years he was a dominant force in developments that changed agricultural practices, the processing of food, and the kitchen habits of the nation. Heinz founded a giant corporation in a new industry, and he carried its products and philosophy to four continents with a promotional flair that probably has never been surpassed.

The diet of Americans in 1869, when twenty-five-year-old Henry Heinz and a still-younger partner named L. C. Noble founded their company, was of a tiresome monotony seven or eight months of the year. The staples were bread, potatoes, root vegetables, and meat, often dried, smoked, or salted. Cucumbers and pickles were the only salad in winter, and in any case, leaf salads were considered unmanly. There was little movement of foodstuffs from one region to another, except for the shipment of meat, and each part of the country had its marked variations and limitations in diet. The grocery store had no produce section; fresh vegetables and fruits were sold in season only. Grapefruit was unknown outside Florida, and an orange was something found in a Christmas stocking. Tomatoes were an exotic Mexican fruit, long grown and admired as "love apples," for which the nation was just beginning to acquire a taste. In the relatively new art of commercial preservation in cans and bottles, the food was laced with chemicals that caused digestive disturbances, if not worse. (The 1911 *Britannica* devoted thirty-two columns to the adulteration of food.)

Henry J. had become a food merchant at the age of twelve, and his first triumph had to do with food adulterants. Living in Sharpsburg, a small town on the Allegheny River six miles above Pittsburgh, he peddled the excess produce of the family garden to his neighbors, first in a handbasket, then in a cart, graduating to a horse and wagon, four acres under cultivation, and thrice weekly trips to call on Pittsburgh grocers. His specialty, however, was horseradish, the pungent white root that was consumed in vast quantities because it sharpened the appetite, made dull food palatable, and supposedly possessed medicinal qualities, especially for grippe and catarrh. Horseradish would keep only if grated, and bottled in vinegar—a chore that made the eyes smart. A local trade had grown up in horseradish, always in green bottles and sometimes with adulterants that looked like, but were not, grated horseradish. Henry J. bottled his product in clear glass and peddled it as the whitest and best-quality root—look, no leaves, no wood fiber, no turnip filler! When sales rose, he filed in his mind the first two of the Important Ideas that were to make him rich. Important Idea Number One: Housewives are willing to let someone else take over a share of their kitchen operations. Important Idea Number Two: A pure article of superior quality will find a ready market through its intrinsic value—if properly packaged and promoted.

By 1875, their sixth year of operation, Heinz and Noble had, in the words of a contemporary analyst, "built up the business with a rapidity seldom witnessed." Already their company was one of the country's leading producers of condiments. They had moved from the two-story Sharpsburg house that served as their headquarters and manufacturing center (it is now enshrined in Henry Ford's Greenfield Villäge, Dearborn, Michigan) to an office and storeroom in the city. They had one hundred and fifty "operatives" in season; one hundred acres of garden along the Allegheny River (thirty in horseradish); twenty-five horses; a business office and vinegar factory in St. Louis; and an annual capacity of three thousand barrels of sauerkraut, fifteen thousand barrels of pickles, and fifty thousand barrels of vinegar. And they had a new contract: a commitment to pickle the produce of some six hundred acres of cucumbers near Woodstock, Illinois.

Despite their apparent prosperity, the partners had overextended themselves and were in serious trouble. The Jay Cooke banking panic had tightened credit, and times were hard. Throughout 1875 Heinz, who owned three eighths of the company, was frantically busy in a scramble to

As a plaster pin or a cardboard placard, the Heinz *pickle was for three decades the country's best-known giveaway and company emblem.*

ALL ILLUSTRATIONS COURTESY H. J. HEINZ CO. UNLESS OTHERWISE NOTED meet payrolls, obtain loans, renew notes, and cover the ever-larger, ever-faster checks that were drawn on him when a bumper cucumber crop came in at Woodstock—one thousand dollars a day throughout October. Heinz endorsed his life insurance as collateral, borrowed from friends, and mortgaged his house, the house he had built for his parents, and his father's brick kiln. All were lost when Heinz & Noble Company filed for bankruptcy in December with assets of $110,000 and liabilities of $170,000. On January 13, with an empty kitchen at home, Heinz called on three grocers "to trust me for groceries on my honor, and I would pay as soon as I could make something after I would get matters straightened up." He was refused. In his private diary (made available for this article) he wrote: "Bankruptcy changes a man's nature. I feel as though every person had lost confidence in me and I am therefore reserved."

The following month his brother John and cousin Frederick, operating with three thousand dollars of borrowed capital, set up in the food business under the name F. & J. Heinz. Henry J. became their manager, with the private understanding that when discharged from bankruptcy he would own half the company. They barely weathered the first year. "Very close run for money," he wrote in August. "Can't see how to get along and not a man or friend will give us a cent, even on chattel mortgage." Pittsburghers had admired his superb teams, matched for size, breed, and color. Now he wrote: "Bought a cheap $16 horse to help us out of a pinch. He is blind."

The upturn came in 1879. The depression was over. The company made a fifteen-thousand-dollar profit; a Pittsburgh bank discounted $2,500 of the company's paper without an endorser ("This is gratifying"); and Heinz gave each of his best workers a fifteen-dollar Christmas bonus "for faithful efforts and good success."

He paid off with interest, out of his salary, a dozen of the names on his Debt of Honor list—his three-eighths share of the old company's debt. He felt prosperous enough to lend a bankrupt friend five hundred dollars with which to buy back his stock at sheriff's sale, and on his tenth wedding anniversary he bought his wife Sallie an oil painting entitled *Sweet Hour of Prayer*.

The Heinz products increased in variety, volume, and reputation: tomato ketchup in 1876, red and green pepper sauce in 1879, cider

Honeymoon, 1869: Henry J. (Harry) and Sarah Young (Sallie) Heinz.

vinegar and apple butter in 1880, and then other "fruit butters," chili sauce, mincemeat, mustard, tomato soup, olives, pickled onions, pickled cauliflower, sweet pickles (the first ever marketed), baked beans with tomato sauce. In April, 1880, Heinz drew up a contract with the pickle growers around La Porte, Indiana, in which he supplied the cucumber seed and contracted to buy the harvest. Important Idea Number Three was born: To improve the product in glass or can, you must first improve it while still in the ground.

In the summer of 1886 Heinz sailed from New York on the paddle-wheel *City of Berlin* with his wife, his sister Mary, and his four children (Irene, fourteen years old, and three younger sons). He took with him six folding chairs, six dozen oranges, two dozen lemons, a bundle of blankets, and, in the hold, several crates of Heinz products. A muscular, energetic little man (129 pounds) with sparkling eyes and bristling red "side choppers," he carried a pocket diary, a notebook, and a steel tape measure, which he whipped out on any occasion for recording interesting heights, widths, and distances.

He landed in Liverpool, looked around, and wrote: "I have learned little in this city which I can utilize in America to advantage." In the two weeks he spent in London he visited, tape measure in hand, the Crystal Palace, the Albert Memorial, and the Smithfield Poultry and Dead Cattle Market. He copied the inscription from John Bunyan's tomb, collected a white pebblestone from the grave of John Wesley, and spoke to a class at a Free Methodist Sunday School. He called on food brokers, glassmen, a pickle factory, a malt vinegar factory, and the offices of Crosse & Blackwell ("an immense house"). The Houses of Parliament, unfortunately, were closed to visitors, "owing to several attempts in blowing up the buildings."

On June 16 Heinz brushed his whiskers, donned his best frock coat (made for him in Philadelphia by an English tailor), and put on a shiny new top hat. He picked up a Gladstone bag containing "7 varieties of our finest and newest goods," hailed a hansom cab on Great Russell Street, where he had rooms, and directed it to Piccadilly Circus. He was calling on "the largest House supplying the fine trade of London and suburbs and even shipping." The gold letters on the window, under the coat of arms, read: "Fortnum

TEXT CONTINUES ON PAGE 33

At the height of his power: the Founder in 1913 with three grandchildren. On his knee is Henry J. Heinz II, present chairman.

The Empire

"The Home of the 57 Varieties," built 1890–98, stood (and stands) on the north shore of the Allegheny River opposite downtown Pittsburgh. At top, Heinz developed the tank-car method of shipping pickles from salting station to factory. He did not believe in low-key advertising.

# of Heinz

The company made its bottles at its Sharpsburg plant just a few miles upriver.

By 1895 the original factory had grown into the major horseradish maker.

Walkerton, Indiana, one of the company's stations for salting cucumbers. A contract to take an unusually heavy Midwestern crop in 1875 caused disaster.

Celebrating two decades of phenomenal growth, Heinz commissioned the painting The World Our Field *in 1899. He had carried his business to England four years earlier; at his death he had "Agencies in All the Leading Commercial Centers of the World."*

32

& Mason, Ltd., Purveyor to the Queen."

He had no letter of introduction. There was, he knew, no Mr. Fortnum or Mr. Mason. A salesman, he must have known, should be calling at the service entrance, but he grasped his bag, marched through the Georgian doorway, and announced in a firm American voice that he was there to see the Head of Grocery Purchasing. When that gentleman appeared, Heinz introduced himself—a food merchant from Pittsburgh in the United States of America—and began his well-rehearsed presentation. At the proper moment he whipped open his bag. The Head surveyed the products, tasted the horseradish, the ketchup, the chili sauce. Heinz readied himself to meet the expected rebuff with a prepared counterattack. He was astonished and perhaps a bit let down to hear the Head say, "I think, Mr. Heinz, we will take all of them."

He began the story in his diary, "1ST SALE IN ENGLAND," and ended it, "I was highly delighted." Perhaps it was on that day that Important Idea Number Four was born: The world is our market.

(Nine years later Heinz rented an office and warehouse near the London Tower and opened his own English branch. It eventually prospered beyond all expectation, became a Purveyor to the Queen, and developed into such an English institution that an American can win a public-house argument today with an Englishman who insists that Heinz is a company born, bred, and headquartered in Britain.)

Home again, Heinz bought full control of the business and in 1888 renamed it the H. J. Heinz Company. He took over some twenty-two acres on the Allegheny River across from Pittsburgh and there built a complex of solid Pittsburgh-Romanesque office, factory, and service buildings. ("The best of everything," he wrote. "Oak posts throughout.")

The stables were especially notable; one reporter called them equine palaces. They were fireproof, heated by steam, lighted by electricity, screened at the windows. The 110 horses were fed, watered, and brushed by electrically operated machinery; their harnesses were carried to and from the tack room on an overhead conveyor. The floor was cork-brick covered with fresh sawdust, and every morning the hostlers used their brooms to make elaborate designs in the sawdust down each side of a center path. A reporter for *American Grocer* declared with awe that the horses actually exhibited pride in their surroundings.

Heinz had seen at close range the bloody railroad riots that followed a 10 percent wage cut in the summer of 1877, first in Baltimore, where he was stranded for a week because of destruction of equipment, and then in Pittsburgh, where forty people were killed and the militia patrolled the streets. ("It is the awfullest looking sight I ever saw. Millions of property burned down.") He observed that public sympathy had originally been with the strikers. He had seen the orderly, progressive, benevolent paternalism of the German factories. He resolved to use what he called "heart power" to build a community of "workpeople" who would feel so happy on the job and so privileged as Heinz employees that they would never dream of rioting or striking. This was Important Idea Number Five: Humanize the business system of today and you will have the remedy for the present discontent that characterizes the commercial world and fosters a spirit of enmity between capital and labor.

He succeeded so well that he won a gold medal at a Paris exposition "for the policy of the firm tending to the improvement of factory conditions." Numbers of favorably disposed sociologists and at least one authentic union leader visited the Allegheny works and reported that Mr. Heinz had indeed solved the class struggle. There was no labor trouble at Heinz—and there were no unions—for forty-five years. The first strike came long after the death of the Founder, when the Depression and New Deal ushered in new ideas and a new age.

Throughout the years there was always a line at the Heinz employment office. If Anna Kurpiewski was hired and joined the other girls—there were nine hundred of them in 1899—she found an unfamiliar set of conditions. She had a private locker with a key; and if she handled food, she was given a manicure once a week. She had the free services of a dispensary nurse, a physician, and two company dentists. She could read in the reading room after hours, borrow books, attend evening lectures or entertainment, take free classes in cooking, dressmaking, drawing, millinery, and singing, use a swimming pool and gymnasium, and sun herself on a roof garden atop the five-story bottling building. She worked from 7 A.M. to 5:40 P.M., which was what girls in other factories worked, but on Saturday she quit an hour early, at 4:40 P.M.

In the five-hundred-seat girls' dining room in the bottling building she could buy tea or coffee for a penny and take it to one of the long tables, where she would unwrap her lunch and listen while she ate to music played on a large organ imported from Germany. She could feast her eyes on a hundred paintings and drawings hung on the walls, of a kind that would give her elevated thoughts, appeal to her finer sensibilities, and exercise a refining influence in her life. Occasionally, dances were held in the Auditorium, though to endow them with a dignified air, they were called promenade concerts.

If Anna had a suggestion on how to do something better, she could drop it into a box and perhaps get a reward or even a promotion. She could take a friend with her to the annual July picnic at one of the parks, reached on a train chartered to carry some two thousand people. At Christmas she watched and perhaps participated in the employees' dramatic presentation in the Auditorium, after which she received a silk umbrella, a silk scarf, or a handkerchief.

The Auditorium, said to be the first in the country built for the benefit of employees, was the masterpiece of the Heinz complex. It had a musical director, 1,200 opera-type seats, a gallery with boxes, and a splendid dome of stained glass. The dome represented the globe, on which appeared the words, "The world our field." Around the base of the dome were inscribed eight of the highest human virtues: Integrity, Courage, Economy, Temperance, Perseverance, Patience, Prudence, and Tact. The walls held a number of fine paintings, including the famous work created in 1880 by John Mulvany, *Custer's Last Rally*, twelve feet high and twenty-two feet long. Between the pictures appeared "mottoes," some of them written by Henry J. Heinz himself: "To do a common thing uncommonly well brings success"; "A young man's integrity in youth is the keystone of his success in after life"; "Make all you can honestly, save all you can prudently, give all you can wisely." And his favorite, which appeared in offices, halls, waiting rooms, and work areas of every Heinz installation: "Do the best you can, where you are, with what you have today."

In an age blemished by child labor, sweatshops, firetrap factories, callous indifference to industrial accidents, and many filthy food-processing factories, people came thousands of miles to see this utopia for workers. All plant operations were open to public inspection. Visitors were given a guide, an orientation lecture, the tour, free samples to taste, and a souvenir to carry away —a small, green plaster Heinz pickle from the "Heinz pickle works." Heinz himself sometimes conducted the important visitors through the plant and often persuaded them to appear before his employees in the Auditorium. Signatures in the Register of Prominent Visitors in the early 1900's included those of Elbert Hubbard (twice), Burton Holmes, Billie Burke, David Belasco, John Drew, Jane Addams, John Philip Sousa, eighteen Japanese businessmen, the Cincinnati Symphony Orchestra, and the Central Committee of the World's Sunday School Association.

The plant tours, of course, were a form of corporate promotion. Heinz had a superb talent for promotion, and he worked it to the limit. The 110 Heinz horses were all jet black, except for two white mares, and they pulled sixty-five cream-white wagons with green trimmings. People turned to look. When the hundreds of Heinz salesmen rolled into Pittsburgh each January in chartered Pullman cars for a week-long conference, the H. J. Heinz Company Employees' Brass Band met them at the station and marched them across town to their hotel. The country's hillsides and trolley cars blossomed with Heinz advertisements. New York's first large electric sign went up where Broadway crossed Fifth Avenue: "Heinz 57 Good Things for the Table." It was six stories high, and the public soon learned that it had 1,200 lights and cost ninety dollars in electricity every night. Heinz never forgot for a moment that he was operating in the country's most fragmented industry, with commercial competitors on every side, or that every housewife who owned a box of Mason jars was a potential competitor as well as a customer. The fight for shelf space in the grocery store, even before the advent of the supermarket and the explosion of brand-name products, was as fierce as anything the commercial world had known. Every Heinz salesman carried in his sample case a hammer for tacking up advertisements and a clean white cloth for dusting off the Heinz goods on the shelves. While dusting, of course, he would try to place his products at end-aisle or eye level and move competitors' products to the back or to the lower shelves.

Heinz had personally hit upon the "57 Varieties" slogan in 1896 while riding a New York elevated train. He was studying the car cards and was taken by one that advertised "21 styles" of shoes. He applied the phrase to his own products. There were more than sixty of them at the time, but for occult reasons his mind kept returning to the number 57 and the phrase "57 Varieties." "The idea gripped me at once," he told an interviewer, "and I jumped off the train at the first station and began the work of laying out my advertising plans. Within a week the sign of the green pickle with the '57 Varieties' was appearing in newspapers, on billboards, signboards, and everywhere else I could find a place to stick it." The capstone of Heinz promotion was Important Idea Number Six: We keep our shingle out and then let the public blow our horn.

His leading instrument for getting the public to assist him in his advertising and promotion was the plaster "pickle charm," which at first was looped to hang from a chain and then also became a pin. Arthur W. Baum, a *Saturday Evening Post* editor, once called it "one of the most famous give-aways in merchandising history." For no good reason except that they were magnificently availa-

TEXT CONTINUES ON PAGE 44

57 Ways to Keep the Workers Happy
Pictorial mementos of Father Heinz's brand of paternalism

A straight-backed young lady in a clean, well-lighted place neatly handwraps a bottle of Heinz relish for the 1905 trade.

"If You Want Pleasure You Must Toil For It"

Known in his time as "The Prince of Paternalism," Heinz gave his workers free medical and dental care, a gymnasium, a swimming pool, roof gardens, a library, free lectures, and lessons in such useful arts as cooking, sewing, and drawing. But these were the rewards of honest labor, as the Heinz motto quoted above suggests; and when the workers were on the job, management saw to it that they kept busy. Above, the boss gets down to the basics of his business, exhorting field workers to greater harvesting efforts. Right, in the bottling room, a hundred girls pack pickles, one at a time, into spotless bottles with a wooden paddle, giving the pickles a pattern and inserting one red pepper where it will show nicely. There is little dawdling, for the girls get a penny a bottle, and it thus takes 12 1/2 dozen bottles to bring $1.50, considered a good day's pay. Twice a week the girls scrub down the room, and hands must be kept meticulously clean. A new girl is given a free uniform; thereafter she makes her own from dark-blue white-striped cotton, which she buys at cost from the company stockroom.

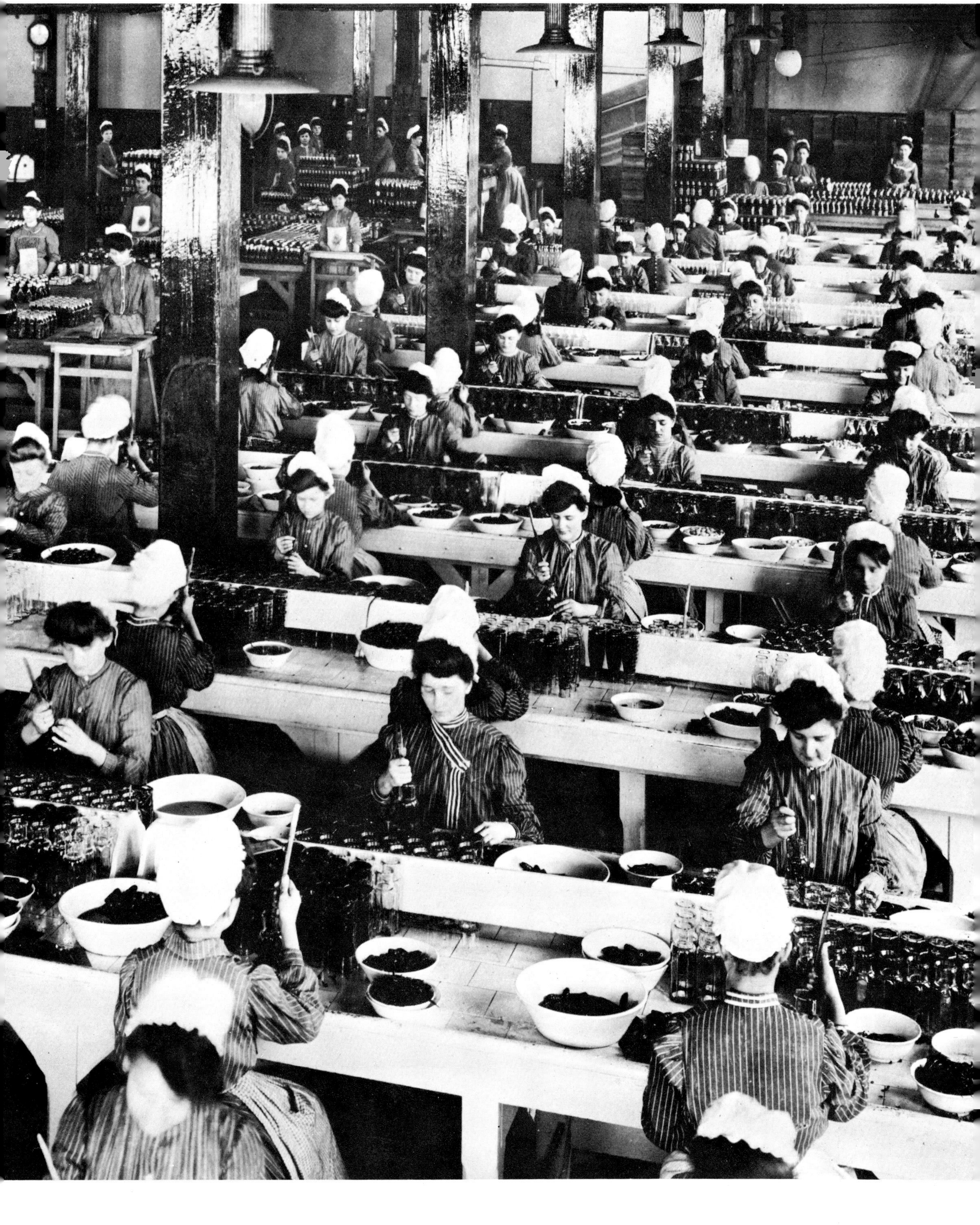

Rewards of Hard Work

When her turn came, a girl worker could climb into a wagonette and be driven elegantly through the city parks. The small building contained the Time Office, where everyone checked in and out, and where all hiring was done. Right, each girl had her assigned place in the girls' dining room, where she had half an hour a day to eat her lunch while she listened to music provided by a talented colleague at the piano. The company had four other dining rooms: one for male factory workers, one each for male and female office workers, and one for top-ranking company officials (male, of course).

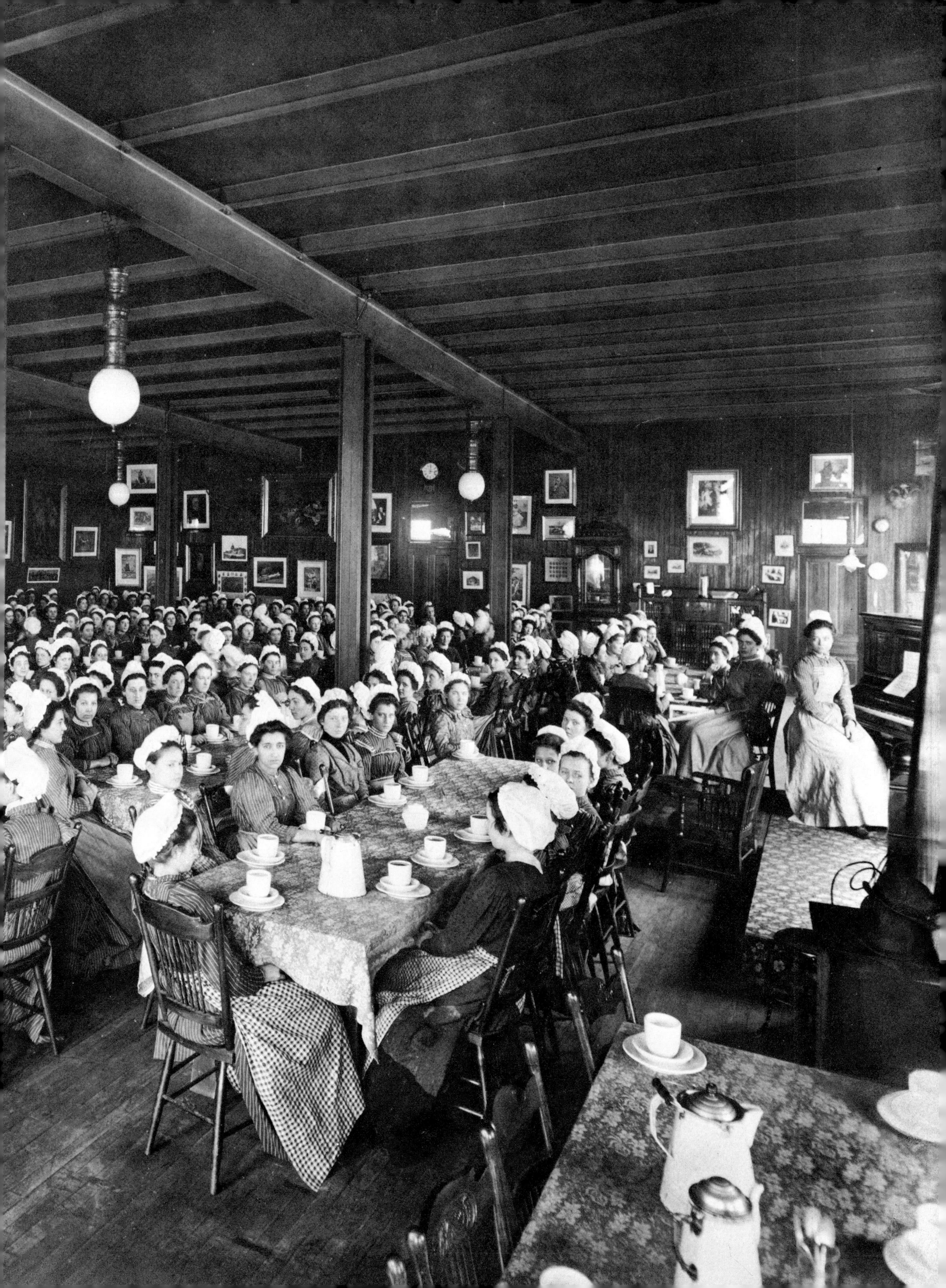

40

*Heinz sales managers, back in Pittsburgh for a meeting, gather in the men's roof garden. (The women had their counterpart.)
The year is 1903, and the bowlers, boaters, and sanguine expressions betoken a life of considerable prestige and satisfaction.
Potted palms and* objets d'art *are tastefully emplaced, and one salesman (rear center) reaches out to express appreciation.*

Nothing But the Best

Above, H. J. with one of his three sons in front of the stables at Greenlawn, his mansion in Pittsburgh's East End. Below, the five-story open rotunda of the administration building, decorated for a reception in 1908. The Heinz Pier (opposite) from 1899 to 1945 welcomed millions of visitors to Atlantic City. Left to right, pictures of Heinz salesmen, display case, demonstration booth.

Orders taken for
A Sample Assortment
Choicest 24 of the
57 Varieties

Heinz was immensely proud of his wagons and prize teams, and used them as an advertising medium in England (top) and the U.S. He bought his first electric truck (below) in 1899, and gasoline cars soon after; but he would have agreed with Winston Churchill that it was a sad day for mankind when the internal combustion engine replaced the horse. Opposite, stained glass windows in the Heinz Auditorium bearing the Founder's mottoes. Circle at center shows the house "Where We Began." The artist who made the windows is unknown, and the windows now have gone the way of all glass.

TOP: COLLECTION OF GREENFIELD VILLAGE AND THE HENRY FORD MUSEUM, DEARBORN, MICH.

ble and that it was the thing to do, a generation of children, an army of boys, wore Heinz pickles on their coats, shirts, blouses, sweaters, caps. Adults carried them for good luck, or as a gag, or because of habit formed in childhood.

Heinz visited the 1893 World's Columbian Exposition in Chicago with his usual pocketful of pins and with plans to give away one million more to the hordes of visitors. The food exhibits were grouped in the Ideal Home Building. The foreign companies—Crosse & Blackwell, Lea & Perrins, Fortnum & Mason, Dundee & Croydon, and others—were on the main floor, apparently on the American premise that if it is imported it must be better. The American companies, including Heinz, were grouped on the gallery at the top of a long flight of stairs. The hordes came, looked through the foreign food exhibits, glanced at the flight of stairs, and left to see other main-floor exhibits, the Midway, and Little Egypt. They had seen the food show and did not return.

Heinz took one look at the straggle of visitors on the gallery and left for the nearest printing shop. He designed and produced a small white card made to look like a baggage check, with the promise on the back that if the bearer presented it at the Heinz Company exhibit, he would receive a free souvenir. His men handed out checks to all who would take them, and up and down the exposition grounds a scattering of small boys dropped them by the thousands. By the thousands the people headed for the food show, swept past the foreign exhibits, and climbed the stairs to the Heinz display. There they viewed an assortment of art objects, antiquities, and curiosities, sampled Heinz products on toothpicks and crackers, and received a green plaster pickle pin. Fair officials had to summon police to regulate the size of the crowds until the supports of the gallery could

44

be strengthened. The foreign food men filed an official complaint of unfair competitive methods. The other American food exhibitors, grateful for the crowds attracted to their own booths, gave Heinz a dinner and an inscribed silver loving cup. He wrote in his diary, "A great hit. We hear it from all sources."

Heinz had two stern restrictions on his advertising: never post billboards in or around Pittsburgh and never advertise in the Sunday newspapers. His successors have lifted the ban on Sunday advertisements, but few Heinz billboards are seen today. One of the last giant outdoor signs stands today in Wenceslaus Square in Prague, Czechoslovakia—a huge Heinz ketchup bottle outlined in electric lights. It remained lighted all during the resistance in the summer of 1968 and throughout the Russian invasion that followed. Czechs have a fondness for the sign; some of them regard it as their window on the West.

The costliest, most ambitious, and probably most successful promotional undertaking was the Heinz Pier at Atlantic City, "The Sea Shore Home of the 57 Varieties," built in 1899 at the end of Massachusetts Avenue and still remembered with gratitude by thousands of foot-weary sightseers. The pier presented to the boardwalk the free-standing façade of a vaguely classical triumphal arch. It was crowned with a broken pediment and (in the early years) had two large green Heinz pickles suspended horizontally and rather attractively between the columns on either side of the entrance. It extended some nine hundred feet into the Atlantic Ocean and had several pavilion buildings at the outermost end. These offered the visitor, free of charge: rest rooms; an auditorium and a concert-lecture series; an exhibition of "industrial and sociological photographs" of the main Heinz plant, its kitchens, and its people; a reading room with writing tables and free souvenir cards and stationery; a kitchen; and at the very end a glassed-in sun parlor. The kitchen had displays of Heinz products ("the kind that contain no preservatives") and offered free samples, cooking lessons, and a place where one might order "a sample assortment of the choicest of the 57 Varieties, which will be delivered to your home through your grocer at a special price, all charges paid. Only one case sold to any one home." The sun parlor held, among other things, an extraordinary collection of 144 paintings, bronzes, tapestries, and curios. Major works among the paintings included *King Lear Awakening from Insanity*, by Hildebrand; *Decadence of the Romans*, by Contour; and *Stanley at the Congo*, by Gentz and Koerner, thirteen by twenty-two feet in size. There were marble busts of Socrates, Caesar, Dante, Michelangelo, Shakespeare, Othello (in six colors), Milton, Louis XIV, Charles Wesley, Napoleon, Garibaldi, and Queen Alexandra of England. There was an Egyptian mummy, a mounted ram's head, a Buddhist household shrine, a framed collection of Confederate money, a couple of nine-foot elephant tusks, a chair made of animal horns with a leather seat, a chair that had belonged to General Grant, and a panel from one of Admiral Nelson's warships. In the forty-five years of its existence, fifty million people visited the Heinz Pier, and every one of them was offered—and most accepted—the Heinz pickle. In September, 1944, however, a hurricane tore the pier apart and cast it into the Atlantic.

In 1905, at the age of sixty-one, Heinz incorporated his company, with himself as president and a select group of relatives and executives as the only stockholders. He was now master of a corporation with eleven branch factories, twenty-six branch houses, and sales in the millions of dollars. He felt a deep dissatisfaction, however, at one aspect of his operation: canning. It still had a bad name, and he was not in a truly respectable business. Commercial food processing did not enjoy public confidence, and it was under increasing attack from the federal government.

The federal attacks were initiated by Dr. Harvey W. Wiley, after 1883 the crusading chief chemist of the Bureau of Chemistry, United States Department of Agriculture. [See "Who Put the Borax in Dr. Wiley's Butter?" AMERICAN HERITAGE, August, 1956.] Wiley had a "poison squad" of twelve young men who searched out and publicized case after case in which processors of food and drink were using harmful chemicals to preserve, color, or flavor their products. From the flank, Upton Sinclair and the other muckrakers were attacking unsanitary and poisonous commercial foods, revealed most shockingly in the spoiled canned meat that had killed American soldiers in Cuba during the Spanish-American War.

Food company executives gave all the arguments why federal interference would be a disaster and all the reasons why the industry itself should be permitted to police its guilty members. Henry Heinz did not agree. He was gripped by Important Idea Number Seven: The food-processing industry will not grow until it has earned public confidence, and the way to earn public confidence is to work in partnership with a federal regulatory agency.

He sent his son Howard to Washington with petitions and proffered his support to Dr. Wiley and President Roosevelt in their program to clean up the industry. Congress passed and the President signed the Food and Drugs and Meat Inspection acts of 1906, which ruled that all foods coming within federal jurisdiction must be prepared in a cleanly manner from pure and wholesome materials and be free from any added substance that might render them injurious to health.

Heinz was now becoming an elder statesman of his industry. He was active in pursuit of such Pittsburgh goals as flood control and smoke abatement (most of which were realized in the "Pittsburgh Renaissance" that began in 1946) and in charitable activities. He was chairman of the executive committee of Kansas City University and president of the World Sunday School Association. He had bought, four years before his wife's death in 1894, a baronial mansion in Pittsburgh's East End, and there he lived with a staff of servants, various relatives, and assorted visiting grandchildren (one of whom, Henry J. Heinz II, is now chairman of the company). He had a conservatory and fruit house (open to the public) and a private museum (open to schoolchildren). He built a settlement house for children in memory of his wife. He travelled to Europe every year accompanied by a valet and a secretary, visited Egypt, Palestine, Mexico, and Bermuda (he met and spent some time with Mark Twain on one of his voyages), and in 1913 took twenty-nine World Sunday School officials on a trip around the world.

Heinz turned much of the operation of the business over to his son Howard (Yale, 1900) and then bombarded him with commanding directives and affectionate reproaches: "I cannot find a single advertisement in the magazines. Are you asleep? Read this to the advertising department . . . careful NOT TO OVERDO IT AT BOARD MEETINGS. Give your partners a chance to say something, and let the majority decide. . . . Our opportunity in California is now. We ought to advertise. . . . You must get outside away from the desk. I wish you would put some competent man to take your place at the desk, and you help to organize other departments. You know you enjoy better health not at the desk, you accomplish more, the results are greater away from the desk, and yet you are determined to stay at the desk.... If I love you I must speak the truth and say the things that will help you."

In sad fact Henry Heinz was experiencing at last an inevitable ailment: he was becoming a superannuated man. His beloved horses had been replaced by Electromobiles and Columbia Electrics, and those were being replaced by gasoline-driven trucks. Howard Heinz was quietly bringing in college-bred chemists to apply scientific methods to the process lines and to do research. One of them, the late Herbert N. Riley, first head of quality control and a vice president, recalled: "In those days the moon was considered as having much to do with the success of food processing.... Every operation was secret and the man who possessed the secret guarded it jealously.... For instance, pickles. It seemed that only men with certain God-given knowledge could successfully salt cucumbers into pickles. They were men of some standing who wore top hats and cutaway coats and of whom the management stood somewhat in awe. The pickle salter was a fellow called Graves. He wouldn't let anyone come into the place. I had to get a special permission or a special order even to let me in to see what was going on. His great thing was to put a finger into the pickle tanks, take it out with a great sweep, shove it into his mouth, suck it, and say, 'Ah, yes, two bushels of salt in *there*, and three bushels of salt in *here*.'

"And spaghetti. I can still see the colorful Italian gentleman in charge of our spaghetti department, specially brought over from Italy, sticking his hand out the window to 'feel' the air to determine just how to adjust his drying process. I got a hygrometer for $400 and that was the end of the spaghetti expert."

Howard Heinz, having introduced the new scientific era to the company's operations, took a leave of absence at the end of World War I to become Herbert Hoover's food commissioner in the Balkans. While he was away, on May 14, 1919, his father died of pneumonia. The Founder, as he has been called ever since, left an estate of four million dollars and many charitable bequests to friends, relatives, employees, and institutions. At his death the company he had started fifty years earlier had 6,500 employees, 100,000 acres in crops, 25 branch factories, 85 salting stations, 87 raw-produce stations, and 55 branch offices and warehouses. It owned a seed farm, factories for the manufacture of bottles, boxes, and cans, and 258 railroad cars. (By 1971 Heinz had companies in many parts of the world, and its sales have exceeded a billion dollars for the first time in its history.)

In recent years, marketing not 57 but over 1,200 "varieties" of food products as it moves into its second century, the Heinz Company has embraced such developments as prepackaged meat, frozen foods, freeze-dried foods, aseptic filling of dairy custard, flash sterilization, computer-controlled processing lines, and mechanical harvesting of fruits and vegetables. Some of these innovations surely would have seemed alien to H. J. Heinz; but just as surely he would be gratified to know that one of his favorite mottoes is still highly regarded by his successors: "Luck may help a man over a ditch—if he jumps well."

Mr. Alberts, our contributing editor, lives in Pittsburgh and has long been interested in the history of the Heinz enterprise.

BOTH: COLLECTION OF GREENFIELD VILLAGE AND THE HENRY FORD MUSEUM

Employees lined the right bank of the Allegheny in 1904, when the house "Where We Began" was floated five miles downriver and enshrined on the grounds of the main plant (third from left). In 1954, crowded by a modern manufacturing building (fourth picture, rear), it was dismantled and moved to Henry Ford's Greenfield Village at Dearborn, Michigan.

Thin as a wire, lively as a cheerleader, Henry Ford does a jig in the cartoon above by Ed Lecocq entitled "Oh, Fiddlesticks," published in 1926 in the Des Moines Register. *The younger set is clearly not with it, or him.*

ALL ILLUSTRATIONS COURTESY OF FORD ARCHIVES, HENRY FORD MUSEUM, DEARBORN, MICH.

THE SQUARE DANCING MASTER

Henry Ford bought a $75,000 Stradivarius, learned to play "Turkey in the Straw," and tried to teach all those Model T riders how to do-si-do like Grandpa

For four decades Henry Ford was one of America's most original crusaders. At one time or another he was protecting birds, chartering a peace ship, proclaiming that every criminal was "an inveterate cigarette smoker," exposing a scheming but fictitious character called the "international Jew," declaring that he would stop making cars "if booze ever comes back," or insisting that only a diet of soybeans, carrots, or wheat could insure good health.

But of all the auto king's crusades, few were more exciting and none created more merriment than his attempts in the 1920's to convince a jazz-mad generation that it was more fun to dance the Virginia reel than the Charleston and to listen to country fiddlers than to saxophonists.

Ford and his wife had organized old-fashioned dance parties even before World War I. But their interest in this form of recreation strengthened after the industrialist's purchase, in 1923, of historic Wayside Inn, in South Sudbury, Massachusetts. There the Fords organized square dances as part of the regular entertainment program. Gratified by their reception, the manufacturer announced in 1925 that he would lead a crusade to bring old-fashioned dances back into public favor.

Organizing an "orchestra" consisting of a violinist, a cymbalist, a dulcimer player, and a sousaphone player, the motor magnate enrolled friends and Ford executives and their wives into classes taught by his Wayside Inn dancing master, Benjamin B. Lovett. Ford's announcement and activities were, of course, gleefully publicized. In an article entitled "Just a Reel at Twilight When Your Flask Is Low," the Cincinnati *Times-Star* reported that "it looks like it will be a big summer for grandma."

To publicize his hobby, Ford invited two hundred Ohio and Michigan dancing instructors to his home town, Dearborn, Michigan, to learn the

Imagine, suggested this 1925 cartoon (from the now-defunct New York Evening World), *the Ford technique applied to the Charleston craze.*

By DAVID L. LEWIS

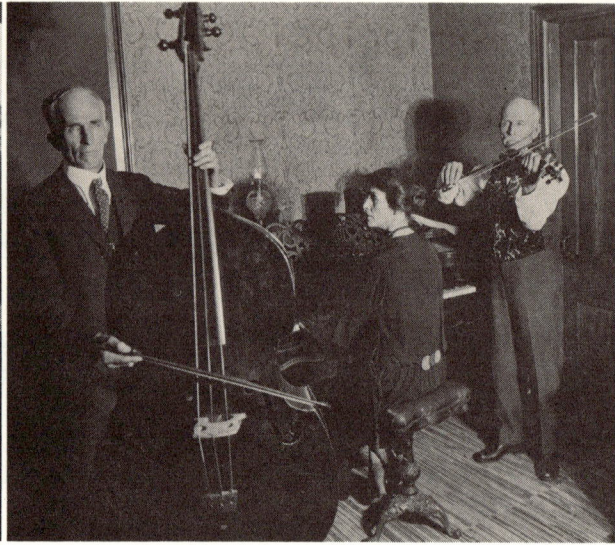

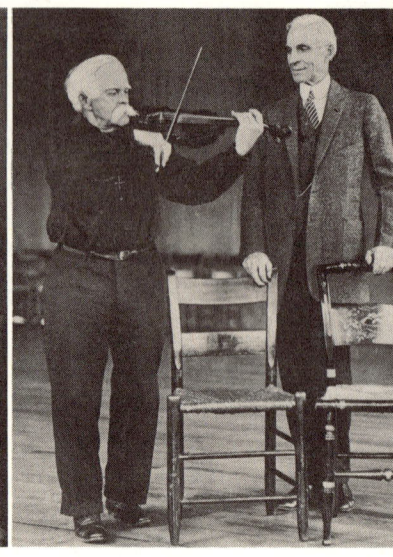

When not dancing, Ford was fond of getting out his Stradivarius and playing with an old-fashioned ensemble. At left, he picks out a tune, accompanied by Clayton Perry (left) on the steel guitar and Edwin Baxter on the dulcimer. The fiddler in the center photograph is Ford's first "find," Jep Bisbee. At right, the auto magnate poses with another "discovery," Mellie Dunham, composer of a tune Ford liked, "Rippling Waves."

Virginia reel, schottische, varsovienne (Ford's favorite), gavotte, ripple, minuet, and other almost-forgotten steps popular in the auto pioneer's youth. He also arranged for his orchestra to play old-fashioned dance music over a nationwide radio network during the public showings of his new cars in January, 1926, and January, 1927. Hundreds of dealers set up loud-speakers in their show rooms and invited townspeople to dance to the music. In some communities nearly 25 per cent of the local populace attended the parties.

In addition, the industrialist made arrangements for Lovett to teach dancing to Dearborn's schoolchildren. After the instruction had begun, two hundred parents petitioned the school board to stop the dances, claiming that they were immoral. Amid nationwide clamor, a jury of five hundred parents saw twenty-five student-couples demonstrate the steps, and voted to have them continued.

Old-fashioned dancing quickly became the rage throughout the country. Newspapers carried detailed instructions covering an entire page. Thirty-four institutions of higher learning, including Radcliffe College, Stephens College, Temple University, and the universities of Michigan, North Carolina, and Georgia, added early American dancing to their curricula; and Ford sent Lovett on a junket to supervise the teaching of the new discipline.

In the fall of 1926 the American National Association of Masters of Dancing, in convention in New York, announced that "the Charleston is dying, the Black Bottom can never be king, and during the past year there has been a great revival in old-time dancing." Henry Ford was credited with the renewed interest in the old steps.

Ford similarly could lay claim to reviving and repopularizing another entertainment of earlier, less sophisticated days—country fiddling. The industrialist himself liked to fiddle, and in his private laboratory would often play "Turkey in the Straw" and others of his favorite tunes on a Stradivarius violin valued at $75,000. To his chagrin, however, he never learned to play well, and he found it quite impossible to dance a jig as he performed. Thus he was delighted when he discovered eighty-year-old Jep Bisbee, who combined both of these talents, at a dance in Traverse City, Michigan, in 1923.

Ford gave Bisbee a sedan and a miniature gold violin set with diamonds, and sent him to East Orange, New Jersey, in his private railroad car so that Thomas A. Edison could film his performance for posterity. For two years Bisbee, who raised his fee from three dollars a night to thirty-five dollars on the strength of Ford's endorsement, was the nation's best-known country fiddler. He was crowned King of Old-time Fiddlers after he had outplayed fifteen other hoary backwoodsmen to win the Henry Ford Gold Cup at a well-publicized Detroit contest.

Jep, however, was quickly relegated to the wings when Ford's next "discovery," a Norway, Maine, snowshoe maker, fiddled onto the national stage. Mellie Dunham, in fact, probably obtained more publicity in the months of December, 1925, and January, 1926, than Fritz Kreisler, Jascha Heifetz, and Mischa Elman received in any ten-year period of their careers. Even the highly publicized Ford stood on the edge of Dunham's spotlight.

The seventy-two-year-old Dunham came to Ford's attention when he won a statewide fiddling contest in Lewiston, Maine, in the fall of 1925. The manufacturer immediately invited Dunham to play at one of his Dearborn dancing parties. Dunham, busily making snowshoes, ignored the letter for several days, thinking it was another order for his handiwork. He was much in demand, having made the snowshoes that Peary's men had worn on their trip to the North Pole in 1909. After opening the missive, Mellie replied that he could not get away for a while because he had to split kindling and patch the barn roof in addition to his regular work at the cobbler's bench.

The Norway *Advertiser* learned of the invitation and published the exchange of letters; the following day "every press association, every newspaper in the country thereupon shouted the news that Ford had a new favorite." Governor Ralph O. Brewster of Maine dispatched a representative to Norway, and Mellie was prevailed upon to accept Ford's invitation.

Dunham left Norway amid the biggest celebration in the town's history. Stores and schools were closed and the citizenry paraded behind Mellie, a brass band, and a police escort to the railroad station, where the Governor and his staff conducted farewell festivities. During the train trip through Maine, New Hampshire, Quebec, and Ontario, the fiddler was hailed at every whistle stop, and the press contingent accompanying him kept the news wires humming.

On December 11, 1925, Dunham played "Pop! Goes The Weasel," "Weevily Wheat," "Speed the Plough," "Fisher's Hornpipe," "Old Zip Coon," and other melodies at Ford's dancing party. The event, attended by a large number of reporters and photographers from Detroit, New York, and Boston, probably was the best-publicized dance in the nation's history. While in Dearborn, Dunham, using Ford's Stradivarius, gave "the most extraordinary recital in the history of music in America."

The fiddler then entrained for New York, where, after remarking, "I came to make some money and I make no bones about it, since me and Ma have had honor enough," he signed a $500-a-week contract with the Keith-Albee vaudeville circuit. Dunham fiddled throughout the United States and Canada for seventeen months, at times receiving as much as $1,500 a week for his services.

In the meantime, dozens of fiddlers throughout the country, including John J. Wilder, President Coolidge's eighty-year-old uncle, came forward to claim they "didn't figure Mellie Dunham was so much of a fiddler," and to challenge him (and Kreisler, Heifetz, Elman, Bisbee, *et al.*) to a playdown. Many of the challengers, including Coolidge's uncle, went into vaudeville, as the nation was swept by a fiddling craze. Contests were held in hundreds of communities throughout the country, and Ford offered a loving cup to many of the winners.

Sheet music and songbooks featuring old-time tunes became best sellers in music shops, and stores handling violins and old-fashioned guitars reported a boom in sales. Horseshoe pitching, wood chopping, marble shooting, and other contests that smacked of the "good old days" sprang up on every side. Ford, as he contemplated what he and his fiddlers had wrought, had every reason to be pleased.

After the spring of 1926, however, the fiddling and the old-fashioned-dancing crazes lost their popularity. Ford, however, was not deterred and continued to hold terpsichorean parties in Dearborn until the early 1940's.

Ruth St. Denis, the great interpreter of Oriental dance forms, was invited to one of Ford's square dances, the flivver king thinking that it would be a treat for her. She attended, but, unable to bring herself to participate in the "remarkable performance," could only sit and sigh, "How awful! How awful!" As for prancing Henry, his form and grace, it was reported, were never better than on that particular night.

The wedding guests admire agile Henry Ford, then seventy-seven, waltzing about the dance floor with his wife Clara, seventy-four, at the marriage of their grandson Henry Ford II to Anne McDonnell in 1940.

Before becoming a professor of business history at the University of Michigan in 1966, David L. Lewis spent twelve years on the public relations staffs of Borden's, Ford, and General Motors. He has published numerous articles on Henry Ford and his company in automotive journals and various other periodicals.

In late February, 1775, three men in what they thought was Yankee farmers' dress, "brown cloaths and reddish handkerchiefs round our necks," boarded the ferry at the foot of Prince Street in Boston, bound for Charlestown, a half mile across the Charles River. At the ferry dock on the Charlestown side one of the "countrymen" dashed forward and muttered something to the redcoat standing sentry (probably "Don't salute, mate!"), for he, like the sentry, was an enlisted man of the 52nd Regiment of the British army; the other two brown-clad figures were officers, Captain William Browne of the 52nd and Ensign [second lieutenant] Henry De Birniere of the 10th. They were bound on a secret mission for Lieutenant General Thomas Gage through what could only be called "enemy country," although fighting had not yet begun. [See "Men of the Revolution—II" in the October, 1971, AMERICAN HERITAGE.]

Gage, who served simultaneously as royal governor of Massachusetts and commander in chief of the British army in North America, had exercised since October, 1774, neither civil nor military control over anything outside of Boston, at that time virtually an island connected to the mainland only by a neck of land about a hundred yards wide. Effective government was in the hands of the Massachusetts Provincial Congress, which was setting about building an army, collecting war materiel, and nullifying the Coercive Acts passed by the British Parliament to punish Massachusetts for the Boston Tea Party.

Gage's situation was humiliating. No courts had functioned in the colony for a year. When the Worcester County court had tried to convene in the fall of 1774, thousands of armed men stopped it, and Gage did not dare send troops to Worcester to protect the court and judges. The "friends of government" (Tories, as they were called by most colonists) were frightened either into silence or out of their homes to army protection in Boston. In the meantime English politicians like the Earl of

By NEIL R. STOUT

ILLUSTRATED FOR AMERICAN HERITAGE BY SEYMOUR LEICHMAN

THERE WAS SOMETHING ABOUT THE
TRAVELLERS THAT DIDN'T SEEM QUITE RIGHT

The Spies Who Went out in the Cold

Sandwich wondered why Gage hesitated to move against such "raw, undisciplined, cowardly men." The Earl told the House of Lords that "the very sound of a cannon would carry them off . . . as fast as their feet could carry them." But Gage knew better. He had been in America for twenty years and had seen the Americans in action; indeed, Gage knew that he owed his life to the Virginia militia when he, leading the vanguard of General Edward Braddock's ill-fated army, was ambushed by the French and Indians in 1755. Gage had a good little army of some four thousand men in Boston, but he said he needed five times as many to be sure of subduing New England. The British government, however, ridiculed his opinion. The General was well aware that he would have to break out of Boston early in the spring of 1775 or he would soon find himself in involuntary retirement.

Gage saw what he had to do. He had already, in September, 1774, sent a raiding party to Charlestown that seized a large portion of Massachusetts' powder supply. But Charlestown was just across the Charles River from Boston, and although no shots were exchanged, the expedition had barely re-embarked when twenty thousand New Englanders were armed and marching toward Boston. Now Gage's informers told him that large supply dumps had been gathered at Concord, eighteen miles away, and Worcester, forty-seven miles from Boston. They were obvious objectives for the decisive blow Gage knew must soon be struck; for to remain bottled up in Boston, or, worse yet, to mount an unsuccessful offensive, would simply encourage the men Gage was already calling "rebels."

Gage's informers had served him well, for the supplies in Worcester and Concord did exist. What he desperately needed, however, was the kind of information that only trained soldiers could give him: locations of roads, river crossings, fortifiable points; sites for encampments; the availability of provisions; and, above all, ways to avoid ambush. Lieutenant General Gage had not forgotten the hard lesson learned by Lieutenant Colonel Gage on the banks of the Monongahela two decades earlier.

For this reason, on January 8, 1775, Gage asked for volunteers "capable of taking sketches of a Country." Most of the junior officers sent in their names. It is not recorded why the two finally chosen were Captain William Browne of the 52nd and Ensign Henry De Birniere of the 10th. Their regiments had come to Boston from Quebec only at the end of the previous October. Browne, however, had probably served in one of the regiments that occupied Boston from 1768 to 1770, and we know that De Birniere was an excellent map maker—his is the best of the maps of the Battle of Bunker Hill. De Birniere also kept a journal, and it is from his careful account that this story is taken.

The General issued orders to Browne and De Birniere on February 22, 1775, to "go through the counties of Suffolk and Worcester [one hopes Gage knew Middlesex County lay between them], taking a sketch of the country as you pass." He suggested that they pose as surveyors and that many "particulars may be learned of the country people," which would seem to be a bad overestimation of Yankee credulity. Otherwise, Gage's orders show a keen grasp of the need for topographical information.

Browne and De Birniere set out the next day, Thursday, February 23, "disguised like countrymen." They would find that it took more than brown garments and red bandannas to make British officers look like Yankee farmers. Fortunately, they had along Captain Browne's servant, an enlisted man named John, who appreciated that fact. Without him the mission might have ended the first day.

From the ferry landing in Charlestown the three spies walked past Breed's and Bunker's hills, past the lane to Phipp's farm (where the redcoats would land on the night of April 18), through "Cambridge, a pretty town, with a college built of brick," and on to Watertown, where the Charles was first bridged. De Birniere noted that Watertown (which had over a thousand inhabitants in 1775) was "a pretty large town for America, but would be looked upon as a village in England." So far, no one had bothered them. A little beyond Watertown they stopped to eat at Brewer's tavern.

This is the first indication of how little information they had about country they were passing through. Jonathan Brewer, the landlord, was a staunch patriot who knew all about British officers; he had commanded a ranger company under General James Wolfe at Quebec in 1759. The two officers sent John off to eat in the kitchen; this must have marked them at once as strangers in democratic New England. Playing their role of surveyors, Browne and De Birniere spread out their maps on the table and called for dinner, "which was brought in by a black woman" whose politeness soon turned to suspicion. One of the "surveyors" observed to her that it was very fine country thereabout, to which the black woman replied: "So it is, and we have got brave fellows to defend it, and if you go up any higher you will find it so."

This disconcerted us a good deal," De Birniere admitted. He and Browne decided not to stay at Brewer's that night. Then they blew the last remnants of their disguise by paying, without argument, an outrageously overpriced bill. Once outside, John told the officers that the woman had told him that she knew Browne was an officer, because she had seen him in Boston five years earlier, and that John himself was a regular. According to De Birniere, John denied it, "but she said she knew our errant was to take a plan of the country; that she had seen the river and road through Charlestown on the paper; she also advised him to tell us not to go any higher, for if we did we should meet with very bad usage."

What to do? They knew now that their disguise would not fool the yokels, and the black woman could have come no closer to stating their mission if she had read Gage's orders. But more than the threat of "very bad usage" from the Americans, they feared that "if we went back we should appear very foolish, as we had a great number of enemies in town, because the General had chose to employ us in preference to them." Armies have always relied on the fact that most men fear the derision of their messmates more than they do the enemy. So they pushed on another six miles. Part of the way they got a ride in a farm wagon, but the teamster and his companion (who they thought was a British deserter) aroused their suspicions by offering to take them all the way to Worcester. They pleaded the need for a drink and got off at the next tavern, the Golden Ball in Weston.

Here their luck improved. The landlord, Isaac Jones, "was not inquisitive." Better yet, when they asked for coffee, Jones replied they could have "what we pleased, either tea or coffee." "Tea" was a kind of Loyalist password, for no patriot would ever offer the hated brew (nor would a Tory, if he had not been sure of his men). Jones put them up for the night and recommended taverns in Framingham and Worcester. He probably also warned the soldiers to be careful about revealing their identities, for Jones had already been given a rough time by the local patriots.

The next day was rainy and sleety, but the spies set out for Framingham, nine miles away. The bad weather helped, for few others ventured out. The soldiers made slow progress, because part of the road passed possible ambuscades that had to be carefully sketched. By the time they arrived at Buckminster's tavern, the three were so wet and dirty that their identities were not so obvious as they had been the day before. Furthermore, they had learned not to send John off to the kitchen, "for we always treated him as our companion, since our adventure with the black woman." They felt safe in Buckminster's inn, so they probably did not know that Joseph Buckminster was a member of the Framingham Committee of Correspondence, a kind of executive committee for the town patriots.

Saturday, February 25, dawned fine. The travellers resolved to push on all the way to Worcester, about thirty miles farther. They took along a lunch of boiled tongue and cherry brandy so that they could avoid going into any tavern where questions might be asked. They made good time, for most of the country was open, and it was not until they were four miles from Worcester that they had to stop to sketch a dangerous pass.

It was five o'clock when they got to their recommended inn in Worcester. The landlord, another Isaac

CONTINUED ON PAGE 100

55

Rosa Parks Wouldn't Budge

In December of 1956 Mrs. Rosa Parks, above, once more rode in a bus like the one in which her impulsive action sparked a year-long, successful boycott.

U.P.I.

A neatly dressed, middle-aged black woman was riding home on a Montgomery, Alabama, bus on the evening of Thursday, December 1, 1955. Her lap was full of groceries, which she was going to have to carry home from the bus stop, and her feet were tired from a long day's work.

Mrs. Rosa Parks was sitting in the first row of seats behind the section marked "Whites Only." When she chose this seat, there had been plenty of empty ones both in front of and behind the "Great Divide." Now they were all occupied, and black passengers were standing in the aisle at the rear.

Then two white men got aboard. They dropped their dimes into the fare box. The driver called over his shoulder, "Niggers move back." Three of the passengers obediently rose from their seats in the black section and stood in the aisle. Rosa Parks did not.

Even when the driver repeated his order and heads turned to see who was "making trouble," she sat as if she hadn't heard. The driver swore under his breath, pulled over to the curb, put on the brakes, and came to stand above her.

"I said to move back. You hear?"

All conversation stopped. No one dared move. Mrs. Parks continued to stare out the window at the darkness. The driver waited. Sounds of other traffic dramatized the silence in the bus.

It was a historic moment: the birth of a movement that was to challenge and ultimately change the social patterns that had established themselves in most Americans' minds as a way of life which was traditional and deeply rooted in the South.

When one weary woman refused to be harassed out of her seat in the bus, the whole shaky edifice of Jim Crow began to totter

Actually, that tradition of racial segregation—loosely nicknamed Jim Crow—was not as venerable as most of its adherents believed. Many segregation laws—especially those concerned with public transportation—only dated from the turn of the twentieth century, and at the start had been resisted, through boycotts, by southern blacks, sometimes successfully. But by 1906 resistance had worn itself out. And in the intervening fifty years the memory had also worn itself out. E. D. Nixon, the man who proposed the Montgomery bus boycott of 1955–56, had never heard of the successful Montgomery bus boycott of 1900–1902. In fact he did not even know that boycotts were again being tried—without much success—in a few southern cities; for example, Baton Rouge.

Nixon was a leader of the Brotherhood of Sleeping Car Porters and one of the founders of both the Alabama state and the Montgomery city branches of the National Association for the Advancement of Colored People. For almost a year before the night of Mrs. Parks's refusal to give up her seat, he had been trying to persuade Montgomery's black community that "the only way to make the power structure do away with segregation on the buses was to take some money out of their pockets."

Few aspects of Jim Crow life were as galling to Montgomery blacks as travel on the city's bus line, which most of them had to use to get to and from work, school, and the central shopping district. There were runs on which a white passenger was a curiosity. Yet the first four rows of seats (ten places) were permanently reserved for whites. And blacks sitting behind those rows could be told to vacate their seats if whites got on after the reserved section was filled.

Blacks also had to endure discourtesy and sometimes hostility from many drivers, all of whom were white. Some used insulting language; others picked quarrels and put blacks off the bus for real or imagined offenses. Some played a peculiarly tormenting practical joke. Since all fares had to be deposited in the box beside the driver, every passenger had to get on by the front door. Blacks then had to get off the bus and board from the rear. The game was to wait until a black passenger got outside, slam the two doors, and drive off, leaving him standing on the curb without his dime.

Resentment was wide and deep in the black community. Some whites, too, were known to disapprove of the bus drivers' harassments. And even among the die-hard segregationists, the mixing of races on a public bus was hardly the emotionally charged issue that integrated schools, or parks, or swimming pools, were. For all these reasons, in the months following the United States Supreme Court ruling of May, 1954, against segregated schools in *Brown v. Board of Education*, black leaders all over the South had been arguing that city bus lines were the next appropriate target for the integration movement.

In Montgomery three individual blacks, all women, had refused to give up their seats when ordered. In each case Nixon and the Montgomery NAACP had vainly tried to rally the black community to some sort of effective protest.

The most nearly successful attempt had been organized in March, 1955, after one of these three, a fifteen-year-old high school girl named Claudette Colvin, had been arrested and removed in handcuffs. An *ad hoc* committee of prominent Negro leaders had called on the manager of the bus company and on the City Commission, which governed Montgomery, to protest the way she had been treated and the whole system that led to such acts of spontaneous defiance. Three demands had been formulated: a guarantee of courtesy by drivers; a first-come first-served seating policy; and the hiring of Negro drivers on runs predominantly in Negro areas.

The proposed seating plan would not have ended segregation on the buses. It only required that when all seats were filled (blacks having seated themselves from the back forward and whites from the front backward), the next passengers to board would have to stand, no matter what the color of their skins. Such plans were in use in other southern cities, and the manager of the Montgomery City Lines was willing to go along with the idea until he consulted the company's attorney, Jack Crenshaw, who declared that the company was obligated to abide by the law, which was "clear on the principle of segregated seating."

In fact, it was not at all clear. Alabama state law did require clearly segregated white and black sections, but the Montgomery city code had a provision that no passenger could be required to give up his seat if another was not available. And there was sound legal opinion to the effect that within the city's limits the Montgomery statute took precedence over state law.

By JANET STEVENSON

Nevertheless, Crenshaw's ruling stiffened the company's resistance. Hope of a legal challenge died when Claudette Colvin's parents refused to let her appear in court. Then community interest cooled to such a degree that the next woman who refused to move back received no organized support at all.

No one knew this background better than Mrs. Parks, who had worked with Nixon on many projects in the NAACP. She could hardly have hoped that her gesture was going to work any profound change in the status quo. She didn't move—as she explained later—because she was "bone weary" and suddenly fed up with being imposed upon. Yet circumstances would render her arrest the spark that lit the fires of resistance.

When E. D. Nixon got home that evening, his wife told him that Mrs. Parks had called from the city jail. Nixon telephoned the desk sergeant to ask about the charges and bail, and was refused the information, as an "unauthorized person." Ordinarily his next step would have been to call a young black Montgomery lawyer named Fred Gray, with whom he had worked on some NAACP cases. But Gray happened to be out of town. So Nixon turned instead to Clifford Durr, a distinguished white Alabamian who had recently returned to private law practice after twenty years in Washington, D.C. Durr had been on the legal staff of the Reconstruction Finance Corporation in the early New Deal years; later he had served as general counsel for the Defense Plant Corporation; and finally he had been a member of the Federal Communications Commission. He and his wife Virginia were part of a small group of southern white liberals who met, with black counterparts, under the aegis of the Alabama Council on Human Relations, to find ways of improving the South's racial picture. Nixon had come to know and trust them both.

"I called Mr. Durr," Nixon remembered later, "and he called down to the jail and they told him what the charge was. Bail was about $50, so I could make that all right." Then Nixon drove the attorney and his wife (who was a friend of Rosa Parks's) down to the jail. "I made the bond," Nixon told an interviewer, "and we got Mrs. Parks out. We carried her on home, and had coffee and talked."

Over coffee, Durr explained the legal alternatives as he saw them: Mrs. Parks could be defended "on the facts." She had not violated the Montgomery city code because there was no other seat available. He thought such a case could be won, but no challenge to segregation was involved. On the other hand, her attorney could challenge the constitutionality of the Alabama state law. That would mean a protracted and expensive battle, with no possible hope of victory short of a successful appeal to the United States Supreme Court. But a victory there would strike a major blow against Jim Crow.

Such a fight would need the backing of some national organization like the NAACP. Above all, it would take all the community support that Montgomery's blacks could mobilize.

Fired by the prospect Durr outlined, Nixon went home and told his wife, "I think we got us our test case at last." As he saw it, Fred Gray would take Rosa Parks's case and "do like Mr. Durr said. Go up all the way!" Meantime, he added, "What we got to do now is see about getting folks to stay off those buses Monday when Mrs. Parks comes up in Recorder's Court."

Mrs. Nixon told her husband he was "just plain crazy." "If headaches was selling for a dollar a dozen," she said, "you'd be the guy who'd go into a drug store and ask the man to put some in a bag." She didn't believe sympathy for Mrs. Parks was going to keep people off the buses "when it's as cold as this, and Christmas coming on."

There was some cause for pessimism. Montgomery's black community of fifty thousand persons was, in one observer's phrase, "as caste-ridden as any country in the world except India." No issue and no leader had yet managed to bring anything resembling unity out of its political, religious, economic, and cultural diversity. There might be strong support for Mrs. Parks in the professional group (made up in the main of faculty members from Alabama State College), but those people did not use public transportation. The working people, who did, depended on the buses to get to their jobs and on their jobs to feed and shelter their families. The risk of losing even a single day's pay was too much to ask of the head of a household already living on the edge of poverty.

But Nixon was determined to ask just that and more. Before he went to bed that night he planned a meeting of some forty people for the next day at the Dexter Avenue Baptist Church, a leaflet calling for a one-day bus boycott, and a Monday evening mass meeting to organize further action. He hoped to find a leader to carry on while he was out of town on his job.

Among the local blacks whom Nixon summoned was the Reverend Ralph Abernathy, a militant young Baptist preacher wholeheartedly in agreement with the plan and eager to get to work. There was also the Reverend H. H. Hubbard, head of the Baptist Ministerial Alliance. The Baptists were the largest denomination in the black community, so Hubbard's promise to cooperate in notifying his associates was crucial, and Nixon was elated to get it. Thus encouraged, he called young Dr. Martin Luther King, Jr., the new pastor of the Dexter Avenue church.

It was a fateful contact. Neither man could foresee that it would put young Dr. King on the road to national and historic importance, a Nobel Prize, and, ultimately, death at an assassin's hand. The future leader was then merely a recently arrived young minister of a fashionable Negro church in a southern town, well educated in the North, with a doctorate from Boston University, but with no other distinctions or activist record. Busy with his new duties, in fact, and the responsibilities of a young baby at home, he had only recently turned down the presidency of the local NAACP, and he told Nixon that while the protest organizers were welcome to meet in his church, he was not sure of his own participation. But he soon changed his mind and, with it, his destiny.

The meeting of more than forty people that afternoon quickly agreed to a one-day boycott of the city buses on the day of Mrs. Parks's trial. When it came to agreeing on demands, however, the initial unity was threatening to dissolve until someone pointed out that demands were unimportant compared to the practical problem of spreading the word quickly. There was no black "ghetto" in Montgomery. Negroes lived everywhere in and around the city. A volunteer phone committee could start work at once, but many black families were without phones—and radios or TV sets—and did not take newspapers. Leaflets, which Abernathy had wanted mimeographed immediately on hearing from Nixon, could be passed out at stores where Saturday shoppers congregated. Announcements could be made from church pulpits on Sunday, provided that every minister in town could be persuaded that the notice was important enough not to be ignored.

Transportation was a more serious problem. The first draft of the leaflet said: ". . . *take a car, or share a ride, or walk.*" But thousands lived too far from their jobs to walk, had no car, and knew no one with whom to share. For them some alternative way of getting to work on Monday had to be found, or the protest would not achieve the 50 per cent cut in company revenues that was the agreed target.

Someone suggested appealing to the Negro cab companies, asking them to pick up pedestrians and carry them to their destination for the ten-cent bus fare. (Segregation was so complete in Montgomery that only cabs driven by blacks and marked "Colored" were permitted to carry black passengers. The eighteen such companies and their 210 black drivers would prove a strong help in the first days of the boycott.)

By the time the meeting adjourned, assignments for phoning, distributing leaflets, and reaching ministers and the cab companies had been handed out, and morale was high. Some optimist even suggested that the passenger load of the bus lines might be cut as much as 60 or 65 per cent! Then, two events took place on Sunday that increased the chances of such success. The first was the result of a Friday encounter between E. D. Nixon and a reporter from the Montgomery *Advertiser* named Joe Azbell. The *Advertiser*, Montgomery's major journal, was seen by everyone, white and black, who read the papers in the city. It was by chance that Nixon ran into the white reporter, whom he knew to be friendly. Nixon told him he would give him a hot tip, but warned: "I don't expect to cooperate with anybody who's going to write some sort of degrading story about Negroes."

Azbell promised to write a useful story, if any. Then Nixon told him about Mrs. Parks's action and the planned boycott. Both men agreed that the story should not be attributed to Nixon, but that Azbell should "find" one of the leaflets on some city sidewalk. Sure enough, Sunday morning's *Advertiser* carried a two-column, front-page story, presumably given to the paper by an indignant white woman who had got it from her illiterate maid. The tone was properly disapproving ("Just listen to what the Negroes are up to now!"). But Azbell had kept the bargain, and as Nixon had anticipated, "every preacher in town saw it before he went into his pulpit that morning," and found it important enough to announce.

The other helpful event was a radio announcement by Montgomery's police commissioner that two motorcycle policemen would be assigned to follow every bus on Monday, "to protect anyone who wished to ride from harassment by goon squads." This, it was believed, had the effect of frightening some waverers away from the bus stops.

It was dark when the first buses began to roll on Monday, December 5. Dr. King and his wife, Coretta, who lived a few yards from a stop on one of the predominantly Negro runs, were up at dawn to see how the prospects for a 60 per cent reduction looked.

The early buses were usually crowded with black domestic workers on their way to make breakfast in white kitchens. Today, the first bus was empty. The Kings stayed at the window until the next bus passed. It, too, was empty. The third had two passengers, both white.

As the sky brightened, those of the planning committee with cars cruised the streets in different parts of town. What they saw was amazing. Sidewalks were crowded with black pedestrians. College and high school students were thumbing rides. Cars driven by blacks were overloaded with ride-sharers. There were a few old-fashioned horse-drawn buggies on the street, and one man was seen riding a mule. Youngsters waved in derisive humor at motorcycle police-

59

men behind most of the buses. Some walkers—with up to six miles to go—sang as they trudged along. As King later wrote in his book, *Stride Toward Freedom*: "A miracle had taken place. The once dormant and quiescent Negro community was now fully awake."

At 9:30 A.M. the drama shifted to the courtroom, as Mrs. Parks's case was called. Fred Gray adhered to the line Durr had suggested. He ignored the conflict of state and local laws, and argued instead that segregation on public transportation was a violation of the spirit and letter of the United States Constitution. Without comment on Gray's argument, the judge found Mrs. Parks guilty and fined her ten dollars and court costs, which brought the total to something like fourteen dollars. Gray announced that his client would appeal the verdict, and she was released on bail. Now it was time for a third act: the mass meeting scheduled for 7 P.M. at the Holt Street Baptist Church.

But first, Nixon and Abernathy talked over the needs of the future.

These included long-term plans and a permanent organization to carry on the fight. Nixon proposed to call it the Montgomery Citizens' Council, but Abernathy thought that sounded like the White Citizens' Councils that were springing up in opposition to school desegregation. His own suggestion was the Montgomery Improvement Association, and Nixon agreed to go along. They also agreed to ask the meeting to approve of repeating the demands made in Claudette Colvin's case—which fell short of total integration. And then, Abernathy raised the potentially touchy issue of leadership. "Brother Nixon, you're going to serve as president, aren't you?"

"Not unless you all turn down the man I have in mind. That's this young reverend, Martin Luther King, Jr."

Abernathy was surprised. King was not only young—not quite twenty-seven years old—but very new to the area. To nominate him would be to pass over a number of other, older ministers, many of whom had good qualifications.

"I'll tell you my reasons," Nixon said. "First, there's the way he talks. Day I first heard him preach, I turned to the fellow sitting next to me and I said, 'I don't know just how I'm going to do it, but one day I'm going to hook him to the stars!'"

King's education equipped him to talk to Montgomery's white leaders in their own terms. King had a reputation for courage, too. As Nixon said, "You knew he wasn't any white man's nigger." And he had not been in Montgomery long enough to become entangled in any of the factional struggles that divided the black community.

Abernathy agreed that King was a good choice, but thought he would decline. So it was decided to nominate him without warning at a session of the "planning committee"—which would frame resolutions to present to the mass meeting. King was so astonished by the very fact of his election—it was unanimous—that he put up no resistance, confessing later that if he had had time to think, he would have almost certainly refused. Immediately afterward he received a tough assignment: presenting to the crowd not merely the routine matters of choosing a name and officers but the hard choice of whether to continue the boycott or merely threaten to renew it if demands were not met. That decision, clearly, had to be made by those who would carry it out: the thousands of humble people who had walked on this cold, gray morning. Many of them would be present at the Holt Street Baptist Church, and they would there be asked to vote on whether they could sustain their incredible initial momentum by approving a recommendation to continue.

By the seven o'clock meeting time there was not a seat empty in the Holt Street church. Loudspeakers had been installed on the roof to accommodate latecomers who might not find room inside. It took Dr. King fifteen minutes to work his way through the crowd from his car, and ten more to get to the platform after he was inside. The audience was singing "Onward, Christian Soldiers" when he joined Nixon, Abernathy, a number of other ministers, Mrs. Parks, and Fred Gray. After the ritual of prayer and scripture reading—with which all such meetings open in the South—and an ovation for Mrs. Parks, E. D. Nixon rose, glancing at Montgomery's police commissioner, whom he saw seated in one of the pews.

"Before you brothers and sisters get comfortable in your seats," Nixon began, "I want to say if anybody here is afraid, he better take his hat and go home. This is going to be a long, drawn-out affair, and before it's over, somebody's going to die."

There were loud amens, but no one reached for his hat. Nixon then delivered a rouser in favor of continuing the boycott, ending with the

Black churches were the morale-building centers and headquarters of the bus boycott. At revivallike meetings Dr. King and other shepherds urged their loyal flocks to persevere.
DAN WEINER

challenge: "We've worn aprons long enough. It's time for us to take them off!"

The next speaker was Martin Luther King, Jr. He came to the rostrum almost completely unprepared for what he knew by now would be one of the most important addresses of his life. There had hardly been time in the two hours since he had been given this task to think through the basic purpose of his speech. His analysis had gone as far as dividing it into two possibly contradictory aims: the first, to drain off the anger of those who were "tired of being kicked about by the brutal feet of oppression"—anger that might lead to violence of which he disapproved; and a second, to "keep them courageous and prepared for action." Or, as he put it in another place, the problem was to be militant and moderate at the same time. To make things more difficult, he would have to face the microphones and lights of television crews, for news of the morning's action had focussed national attention on Montgomery.

King rose to the moment. Pulpit oratory, once a typical American art, is obsolete in most parts of the country today. But it lingers on in the black South, and King's sermon was a classic production. Stating the Christian case for nonviolent protest, he said: "We have been amazingly patient . . . but we come here tonight to be saved from that patience that makes us patient with anything less than freedom and justice." Though he roused his audience at first by shouting, "We are tired. Tired of being segregated and humiliated," he brought them down to calmness again by declaring, "Once again we must hear the words of Jesus. 'Love your enemies. Bless them that curse you. Pray for them that despitefully use you.' If we fail to do this, our protest will end up as a meaningless drama on the stage of history. . . . We must not become bitter and end up by hating our white brothers." And in a final chord, he wooed them to their better selves.

"If you will protest courageously, and yet with dignity and Christian love, future historians will say, 'There lived a great people—a black people—who injected new meaning and dignity into the veins of civilization.' This is our challenge and our overwhelming responsibility."

The audience rose, cheering, and one elderly woman remembered afterward the feeling that she "saw angels standing all around him when he finished, and they were lifting him up on their wings!"

Even before Ralph Abernathy read the recommendation, the verdict was in. It was, in Clifford Durr's recollection, "a grass roots verdict if there ever was one. Some of the [black] middle-class professionals were saying, 'Well, we showed them this morning.' But the maids and the cooks, the ones who had done the walking, were saying, 'We haven't showed them a thing yet! But we're going to stay off those buses until they make up their minds to treat us decently.'"

For the first few days this unanimous determination created a euphoric optimism. In view of the unprecedented effectiveness of the boycott and the willingness of the Montgomery Improvement Association to settle for a partial victory such as first-come first-served seating through separate doors, it was generally believed that there would be a negotiated settlement. But on Thursday, December 8, when Abernathy's committee met with the City Commission, the bus company attorney, Jack Crenshaw, once more insisted that the Alabama law required continued total segregation. City officials were taking a hard line, too. It was clear that they did not want a Negro victory to stimulate further challenges. And a hint was dropped of strong action to come. The city code set a minimum cab fare of forty-five cents per passenger. Negro taxi companies might soon be forbidden to take passengers at ten cents per trip. The next day that threat did materialize. But fortunately, on Thursday evening there had been one of the twice-weekly meetings planned for the boycott's duration as a way of exchanging information, squelching rumors, boosting morale, and ratifying decisions. Anticipating the city's action, the chairman had appealed for volunteer drivers. One hundred and fifty names were handed in. Next, Rufus Lewis's Transportation Committee sat up all night, working out the details of a system which utilized the whole intricate network of black institutions that had grown up under

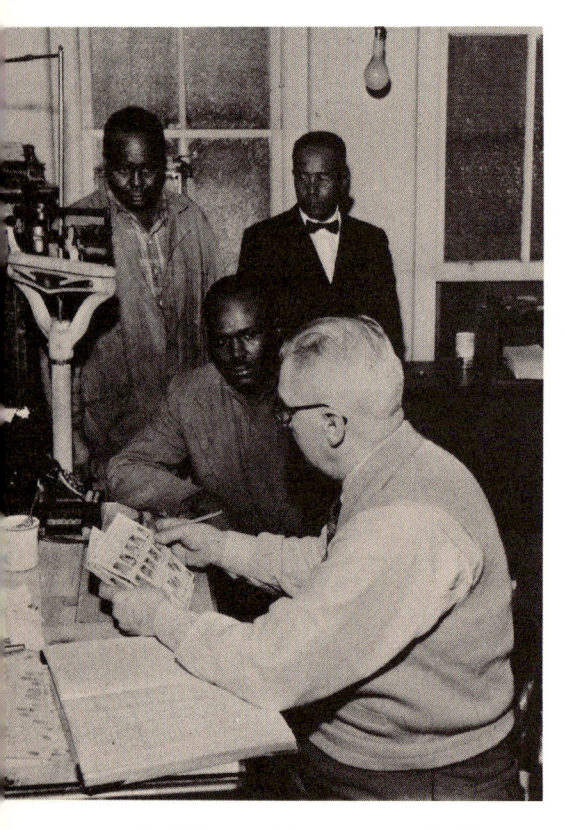

In February Montgomery authorities arrested and booked nearly a hundred people for breaking a state anticonspiracy statute.
WIDE WORLD

the hothouse conditions of total segregation.

On Tuesday, just a week after the first day of the boycott, thousands of leaflets were ready for distribution, showing on a map of the city the location of forty-eight dispatch and forty-two pick-up stations, with the hours at which each would be operative. There were plenty of problems still. Dispatch stations for sending people off to work were easy to locate in Negro neighborhoods, and churches could shelter riders who had to wait in bad weather. But after-hours pick-up stations had to be in less friendly territory. Without the intimate knowledge of Montgomery's white neighborhoods supplied by black mail carriers, this part of the plan would have been impossible to design. There were never quite enough volunteer dispatchers at rush hours. Cars sometimes broke down, and so, occasionally, did the tempers of passengers and drivers. But overall, the car pools worked as well as, if not better than, the old bus system. And their impact as a unifying force in the black community was incalculable.

It was expensive, but help came from two unexpected sources. As the "Montgomery Story" was spread throughout the country by the news media, contributions began coming in to the M.I.A. from cities in the North and West. Black churches took up collections to buy station wagons, which were presented to Montgomery churches of the same denominations for car-pool use.

The load was also lightened by some white Montgomery housewives, who entered into a sort of conspiracy with their black domestics. Accepting the police commissioner's fiction about "goon squads," these women began to drive their maids and cooks to and from work, "to protect them from harassment." When the mayor protested that this gave aid and comfort to the boycott, ladies wrote letters to the newspaper suggesting that he provide them with other help before telling them how to run their households.

As weeks went by without the blacks yielding, threats of violence began to be directed against the leadership of the M.I.A. King, Abernathy, Nixon, and other officers started to receive hate mail and phone calls warning them to "get out of town or else. . . ." Then, on January 30, the ugliness erupted.

On that night, while Dr. King was attending one of the regular mass meetings, a bomb tossed onto the porch of his house exploded seconds later with a shattering roar. Having heard the thud as the missile landed, Mrs. King and a visiting friend had moved quickly toward the rear of the house. They and the Kings's infant daughter escaped injury. But it looked for a time as if the chief casualty of the night would be the concept of nonviolence to which the Negroes had so far been held by their leaders.

Rushing home, King found an angry crowd milling on his lawn. As he stepped from his car, he heard one black man offer to shoot it out with a white policeman who was trying to push him back. Mayor W. A. "Jackie" Gayle and Police Commissioner Clyde Sellers were on hand, along with white reporters and the police. The mood of the crowd was so hostile that all of them later reported having felt that a race riot was a distinct and immediate possibility.

Dr. King went into his house, assured himself that his family was all right, and then came back to speak to the crowd. His voice was unusually quiet, and everyone else stopped speaking or moving, to listen.

"My wife and baby are all right," he told them. "I want you to go home and put down your weapons. We cannot solve this problem through retaliatory violence. . . . We must love our white brothers no matter what they do to us. We must make them know that we love them. Jesus still cries out across the centuries, 'Love your enemies.' This is what we must live by." Then, his voice swelling with emotion, he added: "Remember, if I am stopped, this movement will not stop, because God is with this movement."

It was another miracle of oratory, in a different style from his Holt Street speech. This time there was no applause. Simply, at his request,

"Guilty!" was the bad news for this boycott trial crowd. But after legal segregation's death, the cases were dropped.
WIDE WORLD

the crowd began to melt away, and with it, the tension. King even got them to listen quietly as the mayor promised a reward for information leading to the arrest of the bombers. But it had been a close thing. A small incident could have brought bloodshed. Calm returned, although two nights later a bomb landed—harmlessly—in the Nixons' yard.

After that climactic moment, there was a year-long struggle marked by court actions, by feats of improvisation that kept the M.I.A.'s transportation system rolling, and finally by fresh bombings.

Perhaps the most significant and least publicized action on the legal front was the petition on behalf of the M.I.A. for a hearing on the constitutionality of the Alabama segregation law before a three-judge federal court. This tactic was first suggested by Clifford Durr. About mid-April he realized that something more would be needed than Mrs. Parks's appeal, which was before the Alabama court of appeals, to carry the case to the top. The Supreme Court could not render a decision "on the merits" until the Alabama court had spoken—almost certainly against Rosa Parks. Durr later related what the problem was:

We knew they [the Alabama judges] were going to hold out as long as possible, and maybe never rule on the merits at all. They could reverse the lower court on some narrow technical ground and send the matter back for a new trial, and it could just drag on forever. Meanwhile, the city authorities were getting ready to break up the car-pools. They'd found some grounds for an injunction and if it was granted, that meant the end of the boycott. People just couldn't afford to give up their pay checks—not the people who were the backbone of the movement, who had low wages and large families and no savings to live off of.

Durr therefore suggested to Fred Gray that he petition for a special three-judge federal court and ask it for an injunction against discrimination in seating, on the grounds that it was a violation of rights guaranteed in the Constitution. Such a panel was allowable in a federal action challenging a state law. And its rulings could be appealed directly to the Supreme Court.

Gray went to work at once, made contact with the New York and Washington branches of the NAACP, got some high-powered co-counsel, and filed his petition. The hearing was set for early in May. The court was composed of Richard T. Rives, at the time judge of the United States Circuit Court for the district including Alabama, who was the presiding justice; Judge Frank Johnson, an indigenous "Andrew Jackson Republican" (in Durr's words) from the northern part of Alabama; and Judge Seybourne Lynn of Birmingham.

Within three weeks, two of the three white southern judges—Johnson and Rives—outvoted their colleague and ruled in favor of Gray's petition. Rives, who wrote the majority opinion, was threatened, obliged to listen to sermons attacking the federal judiciary in the Montgomery church he attended, and had garbage dumped on his son's grave in a local cemetery. Johnson took similar abuse. But the strategem was successful.

The federal question was raised at last. For the city of Montgomery appealed the ruling "on the merits," and the state of Alabama joined in the appeal; the matter now went onto the Supreme Court's docket.

That made the third case arising out of the bus battle to be working its way through the judicial system. The first was Mrs. Parks's appeal. Then, in March, a second had arisen when King and other M.I.A. leaders had been found guilty of violating a state antiboycott injunction—in a trial that usefully exposed black Montgomeryites' grievances to the national public. Their conviction, likewise, was on appeal.

Montgomery authorities were meanwhile harassing the car pools. A car full of riders would be flagged down; the inspecting officer would find one or more violations of the state safety standards—weak brakes, poorly aligned headlights, or something else. The driver would be forced to abandon his vehicle, and a city wrecker would be called to tow it away (at the owner's expense) for repairs (also at his expense) in a city-approved shop. A similar tactic was the arbitrary cancellation of black auto-owners' insurance.

But all this was only prelude to the main attack. On October 30 Mayor Gayle directed the city's legal department to request an injunction "to stop the operation of the car pools or transportation systems growing out of the bus boycott," and to collect damages of fifteen thousand dollars for loss of tax revenues. Fred Gray's counterpetition to prevent the city's interference on behalf of the bus company was denied. A hearing was set for November 13.

There was no question in the minds of the M.I.A. leaders that this was, as King confessed to a mass meeting on the second of November, a bad moment. The city was certain to get its injunction, and to end the car pools would hopelessly undercut the boycott. He tried to rally confidence by saying, "This may well be the darkest hour before dawn. We have moved all these months with ... daring faith.... We must go on with that same faith...."

November 13 found the main contestants on both sides in court for the injunction hearing. The same judge who had tried Mrs. Parks a year earlier was listening to the arguments when, some time around noon, there was an interruption.

The two attorneys for the city, the mayor, and the police commissioner were all called out of the court, and there was an excited buzzing at the press table. One of the reporters brought over to the defense table a copy of a message just received over the wire service teletype machine:

The United States Supreme Court today affirmed a decision of a special three-judge U.S. District Court declaring Ala-

CONTINUED ON PAGE 85

64

THE WPA'S AMAZING ARTISTIC RECORD OF
American Design

Ship's sternpiece with American flags, eagle, and seal

From the winter of 1935–36 until shortly after America's entry into World War II, hundreds of artists were engaged throughout most of the nation in compiling a graphic record of surviving artifacts from the American past. Antiques shops and old farmhouses, private collections, historical societies and museums, California missions and Shaker barns, were ransacked for evidence that would accurately and colorfully picture the story of our early arts and crafts. The program, organized under the Works Progress Administration, was aimed at maintaining and improving artistic skills that were languishing in the trough of the Great Depression for lack of employment. The Index of American Design that resulted from that program is the most extraordinary and most comprehensive collection of its kind in the world. (It is now in the custody of the National Gallery in Washington.) At their best these fascinating renderings are more revealing than photographic records.

Although this was make-work, it had other aspects. With bewildering suddenness, the almost mystic sanctity of American prosperity had been violated by the stock-market crash of 1929. The nation was completely unprepared for the suffering that followed. It seemed like some outrageous, inexplicable prank of nature that had turned the American Dream into a nightmare. Out of the ensuing bafflement arose a need to understand what was valid in American experience—a search for something more basic and durable than the euphoric aberrations of the 1920's. And in these drawings it was possible to recapture the vitality and warmth of everyday life in earlier, saner times. There has long been a need for wide distribution of this pictorial information. This purpose will be substantially served by *The Treasury of American Design*, a two-volume work prepared by Clarence Hornung, to be published in the fall of 1972 by Harry N. Abrams, Inc. The reproductions herewith are selected from the eight hundred and fifty illustrations in these books.

By MARSHALL B. DAVIDSON

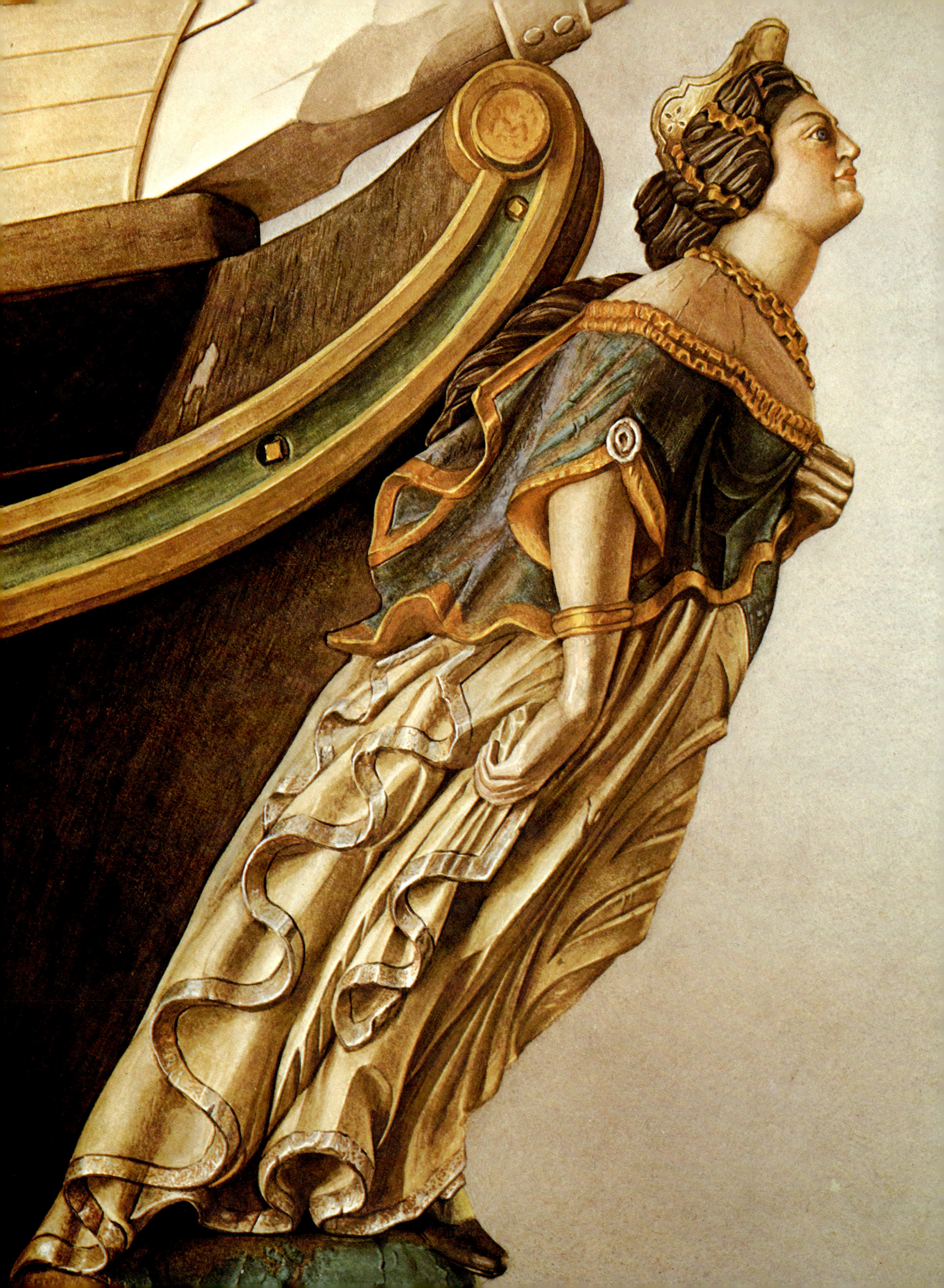

FACE TO THE SEA

In America the art of the sculptor was deeply rooted in the craft of the woodworker. Long before native artists began to chisel their images from marble and cast them in bronze, generations of wood carvers had displayed their considerable talents fashioning portraits and other figures from local timber. And long after the more sophisticated American sculptors were earning fair reputations in the world of the fine arts for their work in stone and metal, contemporary artisans continued to shape effigies in wood that were both decorative and useful. None maintained that tradition more vigorously than the carvers of ships' figureheads, and few American ships ventured forth without some colorful figurative symbol to breast the waves.

(1) Oak figurehead from a barque, about 1840; (2) fashionable lady, with flowers, from the ship Creole, *built 1847; (3) effigy of Daniel Webster, about 1840; (4) eagle head from the* Great Republic, *launched at Boston in 1853.*

(1)

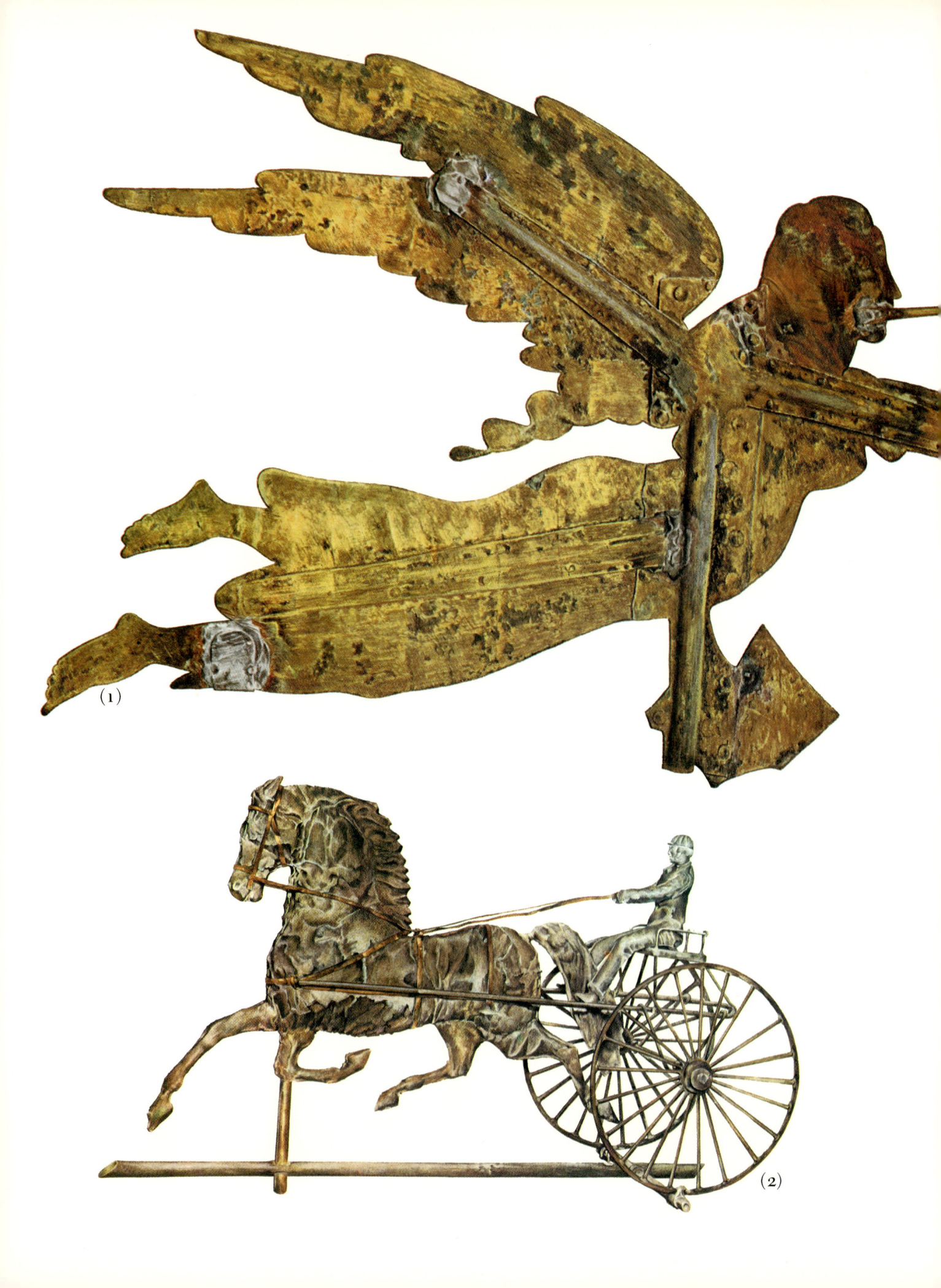

(2)

ART IN THE SKY

Until late in the nineteenth century, America remained a predominantly rural nation where the look of the sky and the way of the wind were matters of constant concern to the countryman. The ingenuity and imagination of craftsmen found their freest expression in designing the weather vanes atop buildings across the land. (Picasso once remarked that cocks—commonly used above churches to recall Peter's denial of Christ—have never been so well seen as in American weather vanes.) Vanes of infinite variety were whittled, forged, cut, and cast into shapes that provided a sort of glossary of American interests and enthusiasms over the years. *(1) Gilded iron vane representing the angel Gabriel blowing a copper trumpet to summon the faithful, made by Gould and Hazlett, Boston, 1840; (2) sulky and driver, about 1875; (3) glass-eyed fish; (4) wood-burning locomotive and tender; (5) late nineteenth-century vane of an* abattoir.

THE PRIDE OF FIREMEN

Service in early American fire companies was voluntary and without pay; formal membership was a distinction, although the young men who actually "ran with the machine" for excitement were often toughs who fought with men from rival companies before bothering with the fire that meanwhile blazed on. Association with a company was a matter of pride that was reflected in the artistry lavished on equipment and regalia—embellishments that were usually paid for by the firemen themselves or by their friends. *(1) Fire marshal's trumpet, silver-plated nickel, 1877; (2) leather fire bucket; (3) hose reel built for the Neptune Hose Company, Philadelphia, 1831; (4) hose holder in the form of an eagle; (5) decorated hand pumper built by Patrick Lyon for the Pennsylvania Fire Company, No. 22, of Philadelphia in 1806; (6) fireman's hand-painted stovepipe hat worn in dress parades.*

THE LEGACY OF SPANISH HORSEMEN

(1)

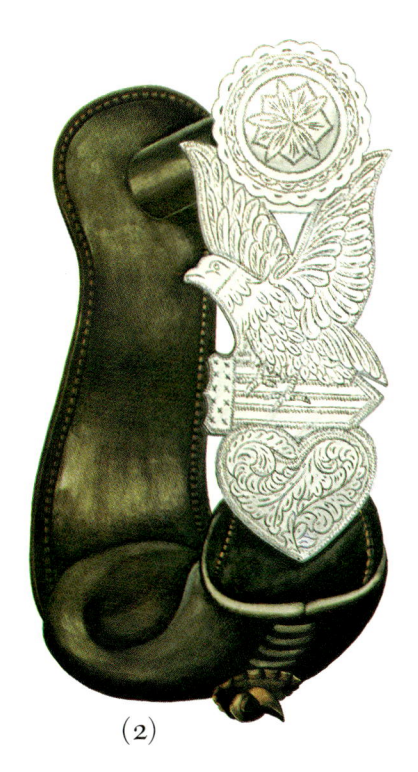

When he visited the West Coast in the 1830's, Richard Henry Dana thought that the Californians seemed always to be on horseback and that they were the world's finest riders. "They are put upon a horse when only four or five years old . . .," he wrote, "and may almost be said to keep on him until they have grown to him." Horsemanship in the Southwest was virtually a necessary accomplishment, and a matter of pride. Saddles, bridles, bits, spurs, and the other trappings were highly personal expressions of taste and pretension. The individual design and the elaborate ornamentation of such gear reflected skills of ancient tradition that reach far back into Spanish history. *(1) Child's sidesaddle with velvet upholstered seat embroidered in silk, probably made in Monterey, California, about 1820; (2) oxbow stirrup with chased silver design of an American eagle; (3) spur with decorated leather strap, silver mounted iron shank, and rounded prong; (4) hackamore bit with leg-shaped side pieces decorated with brand marks on a silver band between outlines of female nudes and equally dangerous serpents.*

73

CIRCUS PARADE

In the last quarter of the nineteenth century the circus flowered in its full glory. People of all ages, all colors, in all sections of the land, eagerly awaited the grand parade into town that was the opening act of the seasonal visit. "It was India and Arabia and the jungle to us," Hamlin Garland recalled from his prairie childhood. "History and the magic pomp of chivalry mingled in the parade of the morning.... It was our brief period of imaginative life." After the show was over, he added, "the memory of its splendors went with us like a golden cloud." Among the popular arts of America nothing quite matched the extravagance and brilliance of circus-wagon ornament that lured the eye and fired the imagination with images of boundless invention. During the season such caravans found their way to hamlets even too obscure and far away to attract a trolley car.

(1) The "United States," one of the most resplendently and skillfully decorated of all circus wagons; (2) carved lion from a Sparks circus wagon, about 1900; (3) draped female figure with a lyre, from a Barnum & Bailey wagon made about 1880 by the Sebastian Wagon Company and possibly carved by Samuel Robb.

(1)

(2)

(3)

THE SILENT TOBACCONISTS

(1)

(2)

With the passing of wooden vessels some carvers turned from modelling ships' figureheads to fashioning shop figures. Until ordinances in many crowded communities prohibited such "obstructions and hazards to passing pedestrians," effigies of almost every race and type known to man could be spotted along city streets—ladies of fashion, race-track touts, turbaned Turks, kilted Scotsmen, and, most endearing of all, cigar-store Indians in the form of braves, squaws, and occasionally papooses. Less than a century ago that mighty, brightly painted tribe of silent, native advertising agents numbered in the tens of thousands. Surviving members in good condition command high prices in today's auction houses.

(1) A typical cigar-store Indian princess, bedecked with feathered headdress and holding cigars in one hand and a plug of tobacco in the other; (2) a so-called white-type (other than Indian) tobacconist's figure of a dude; (3) a Highland chief in the full regalia of his clan; (4) a daring variant of the tobacconist figure in the form of a Gay Nineties belle exposing her limbs to allure the passers-by.

(3) (4)

77

TRADE'S GRAVEN IMAGES

Early in the nineteenth century it was reported that in the art of woodcarving, Samuel McIntire of Salem "had no rival in New England." Aside from his figures in the round, his relief carvings added distinction to the finest furniture and buildings constructed in his day. His equally skilled Philadelphia contemporary, William Rush, carved, among numerous other things, enlarged models of human organs for display in professional anatomy classes. Later in the century artisans often plied their craft in anonymity for less exacting clients. The primary requisite for the trade signs they produced was to illustrate their message in the most direct terms.

(1) Panel displaying the arms of Massachusetts, by McIntire; (2) figure of a manacled felon for a jail; shop signs of (3) a butcher, (4) tailor, (5) optometrist, (6) glovemaker, (7) cobbler, (8) ship chandler, (9) barber.

(5)

(6)

(7)

ROCH THE TAILOR

(8)

(9)

SIGNS FOR WAYFARING STRANGERS

Throughout the colonial period and for years after, little if any distinction was drawn between the crafts and the fine arts in this country. Painters with no formal training or serious practice in art limned the features of their neighbors as a sideline to such workaday jobs as producing ship and tavern signs. Conversely, professed artists of acknowledged talent as readily turned from taking likenesses of their neighbors to producing signs and similar decorations for ship and home and public place. Whatever the level of its artistry, the painted panel that hung before a wayside inn was a welcome sight for the stagecoach passenger. Until the day of railroads and then macadamized turnpikes, overland travel had few rewards beyond the simple satisfaction of reaching a destination in one piece. In 1791, when President Washington undertook a necessary southern tour, Jefferson wrote him: "I shall be happy to hear that no accident happened to you in the bad roads...."

(1) Sign of David Reed's tavern, established in 1797 and featuring entertainment along with victuals; (2) sign of a stage office, 1828, depicting a typical open coach of the period.

A NOTE TO MEMBERS OF THE AMERICAN HERITAGE SOCIETY

The Treasury of American Design will be published this autumn by Harry N. Abrams, Inc., at a retail price of $50 for the two-volume set. Arrangements have been made, however, for members of the American Heritage Society to receive copies at a substantially lower prepublication price. Details will be mailed out shortly. Interested members may write to Martin Rapp, American Heritage Publishing Company, Inc., 551 Fifth Avenue, New York, N.Y. 10017.

Michigan Boyhood
CONTINUED FROM PAGE 7

Whether or not they survived to tell about it, the French filtered more and more deeply into the back country; and if some of them had their troubles with the Indians, some of them got the Indians to help them. Father Marquette, the saintlike little Jesuit who went the length of Lake Michigan and down into the Illinois country for the greater glory of God, had Indian helpers, and when he fell mortally ill on his way back toward Michilimackinac, where Lake Michigan meets Lake Huron, it was his Indian helpers who made his last moments easy, buried him on a sandy promontory, put up a cross to mark his grave, and then slipped away northward to bear news of his passing. Later on they returned to collect his bones and take them back to the straits for Christian burial. (The towns of Ludington and Frankfort today have heated argument about the site of his death. One marker identifies the place at the entrance to the Ludington harbor, and another marker makes similar identification at the entrance to the Frankfort harbor; and learned expositions support each claim.) Obviously, not all the Indians were hostile; in a noncommittal way, some of them were quite friendly.

These Michigan Indians after all were not quite like the tribes farther east. They lacked the incredible, breath-taking ferocity of the Iroquois, for instance; and although as primitive men they carried their passions near the surface and were quite capable of putting captured enemies into the fire if the mood possessed them, they never quite made a hideous ritual out of it in the Iroquois manner, deriving ecstasies from the infliction of pain and going to fantastic lengths to prolong the victims' suffering so that the general orgy that followed the final gasp might have maximum dimensions. They were tough enough, to be sure. The Chippewa actually muscled the Sioux tribes out of the western Lake Superior country, and under the Ottawa chief Pontiac various associated tribes nearly drove the British out of the whole Great Lakes area, destroying the forts at St. Joseph and Michilimackinac and laying a long siege to the fort at Detroit. Later on, when the Americans fought the British for possession of the lakes country, the Indians fought effectively on the British side, overwhelming the outpost at Chicago and slaughtering its garrison, and committing a famous massacre of prisoners along the river Raisin in southeastern Michigan. Anyone who fought these Indians knew that he had been in a war.

Yet the memory of terror, the ever-present dread of the sudden blow in the darkness—the blend of fear and hatred that led otherwise well-intentioned Christian men to believe that the God of love would be pleased if all Indians were exterminated outright—never quite became part of the Michigan heritage. The American settlers dispossessed the tribesman as completely here as anywhere else, but they did not slaughter him while they were doing it. They did not have to; they were not afraid of him, and if the red man was there to be trodden on, he did not have to be kicked first.

Probably there were two reasons for this. To begin with, white settlement came mostly after the Indians' power had been broken. There were very few white-man's towns or farms until Pontiac and the baleful chief Tecumseh had been beaten, and hardly any of the men who made productive clearings in the wilderness ever had to worry about people who might come at them out of the darkness with scalping knives and fire arrows. The long haunted years known to the settlers in Massachusetts and Virginia were not duplicated here.

Even more important was the fact that here the white man reduced the Indian to impotence simply by touching him. The newcomers corrupted him not by intent but just by living beside him. Indian society began to come unravelled not long after Etienne Brulé went to whatever fate he finally got, and it kept on unravelling until it fell completely apart. Exposure to the complexities of European civilization was too much for it. The red man had to adjust every aspect of his life to a scale of values he could neither understand nor control, and it was too much for him. He could not make the adjustment, and he could not conceivably keep from trying to make it.

This was so because the white men offered, for a price, material goods that the Indian wanted—things like knives and hatchets made of steel in place of implements of chipped stone; brass kettles in place of birch-bark buckets; needles and fishhooks and awls made of metal instead of splintered bone; woolen cloth for blankets and clothing instead of crudely dressed skins or mats woven of pounded bark fibers; guns and bullets and gunpowder to replace bows and arrows. Along with these riches, offering life a dimension primitive man had not dreamed of before, there were brandy and rum, strengthened by abominable additives until they almost reached the level of outright poison, which passed into common speech under the accurately descriptive name of firewater. No power on earth could keep the Indian from trying to get these things once he got acquainted with them, and he was willing to pay any price that might be demanded.

The demanded price, of course, consisted of furs. The Indian set out to get the furs, and that was what turned his life upside-down. He became a hired hand for the invaders, and so passed from his own society into theirs before he knew that anything was happening to him; he was the market for the factories of England and

81

France, and at the same time he was the source of supply for an industry that reached from the uncombed trader at Michilimackinac to the richest shops in London and Paris, with a vast network of warehouses and middlemen and cargo vessels lying between. Stone Age man abruptly found himself part of an infinitely complex society, no single phase of which lay within the range of anything he could hope to comprehend. What men made or bought and sold on the far side of an ocean he had never seen laid down the conditions of his existence. Over many centuries he had adjusted himself to the mysterious wilderness where he lived, and suddenly the ways of life and the habits of mind that came out of that adjustment meant nothing at all. Without wanting anything of the kind to happen, he had become part of a culture that had no more than a temporary, marginal place for men like him, and there was no way on earth for him to get out of it.

For several generations the process was gradual, almost imperceptible, and it was fairly painless. The seasons came and went as they always had, the canoe brigades came and went with dripping paddles and red-sashed voyageurs, and the Indian went up the rivers and into the forests to exercise his skills, so on the surface nothing much had changed; yet there was some premonition of disaster, or men like Pontiac and Tecumseh could never have persuaded the tribes to take to the warpath. The warpath was followed, and it led to utter defeat, and shortly after this several things happened, the sum of them meaning outright catastrophe. The Michigan country became trapped out, so that the furs that were the price of life became harder and harder to get. At the same time the fashions that dictated the scope and speed of the fur trade began to change. At the moment when beaver and marten pelts became ruinously scarce they became worth less and less, and the Indian was pauperized through no fault of his own. When white men took the trouble to offer advice, they told the Indian that he must take up the white man's way—that is, he must work for wages at whatever jobs might be available, or he must become a farmer and produce crops for a market that was erratic and as mysterious as the market for furs.

Not many jobs were available at that moment in the land of the Great Lakes, and there was little in the red man's background to fit him for any of them. He could become a hanger-on around the docks of the new seaports, helping to load cordwood on steamboats, or he could do odd jobs here and there—for a storekeeper, perhaps, or a mill owner, or someone similar—but such work was scanty and seasonal, and there was nothing in the Indian's frame of reference to give it any meaning. Farming was not much better. The Indian knew how to cultivate the garden plot that provided him with corn and beans and squash to supplement his diet of fish and game, but raising crops for the market was something else again. Most of the country he was supposed to farm was covered with trees, and when the trees were removed, this timber country offered some of the poorest farming land in North America, as a great many white farmers learned to their cost a little later.

So there was little for the Indian to do except go to seed, which mostly he did with bewildered resignation. He had solved the problem of life in the wilderness, which is to say that he had worked out a culture that enabled him to keep his self-respect and put him in rough harmony with the world he lived in. Now life presented him with problems that were not only beyond solution but beyond his understanding.

At this point the white man stepped up the pace. What he proposed to conquer was not the Indian but the wilderness. He was attacking the earth itself, and his only real concern with the Indian was to keep him from being an obstacle. To be sure, by the second decade of the nineteenth century the Indian in the Michigan country was dying on the vine; but the Americans who had designs on the land had intricate laws concerning the land and its use, and these laws required the composition and registration of numerous pieces of paper. Land titles, in short, had to be cleared. The Indian had never heard of such things, but according to the white-man's law the red man held the title to all of this land, and he had to be persuaded to surrender it. And in the years just before and shortly after 1820 Lewis Cass took care of that.

Cass was one of the notables of the early Middle West. He was governor of Michigan Territory in the days before statehood. Later he became a member of the United States Senate, still later he was an unsuccessful Presidential candidate against Zachary Taylor, and he served finally as Secretary of State in the Cabinet of James Buchanan, eyeing with stony disapproval the convolutions of Buchanan's course at the time when the rising issue of slavery was being so clumsily evaded and resigning, at last, a few months before the Buchanan administration ingloriously ceased to be. One of Cass's minor misfortunes was that the art of photography did not develop until he was well on in years; the portrait by which he is remembered was taken when he was old, and it shows an unhappy face with sagging cheeks and eye pouches and a twisted mouth, the eyes having the look of a man who finds the world gone out of alignment.

Anyway, in 1820 Cass led a small flotilla of canoes up from Detroit, cruising along the western shore of Lake Huron, going on up the St. Marys River as far as the rapids, portaging over the height of land to Lake Superior, following the dangerous south shore all the way to the western tip of the lake, going overland by difficult portages to the headwaters of the Mississippi, descending that stream to the outpost of Prairie du Chien, and coming back across what is now Wisconsin to Green Bay. After a brief pause there for reorganization, Cass went down Lake Michigan to Chicago, then an inconsiderable military station and trading post, from which point he made his way cross country to Detroit, while the flotilla went up along the east shore of the lake to Mackinac and came down Lake Huron by the same route it had used on the way out. All in all, Cass and his men had made quite a trip—four thousand miles or more, up and back, one of the great feats of exploration in American history, done competently and without fanfare under conditions of hardship and peril.

Hardship and peril in full measure, certainly. Travelling the Great Lakes by birch-bark canoe was risky business. The canoes that carried men and supplies were exceedingly frail and would inevitably be twisted into fragments if they were caught in rough water. Inasmuch as the lakes can be as vicious as the North Atlantic when the winds come up, this meant that the expedition had to stay close to the shore all the way, running into the beach and hauling the canoes up beyond reach of the surf whenever the breezes stiffened. To make a traverse across the mouth of an open place like Saginaw Bay, or to cruise along the pictured rocks in Lake Superior with no shelving beach anywhere near, was to risk the lives of every man in the party. Repeatedly they had to camp for two or three days at a time waiting for better weather. Every mile of the way Cass and his men had to carry the certain knowledge that in case of disaster there was no help anywhere within reach. They were on their own.

But there seem to have been compensations: chiefly, a sense of wonder, because this unstained new country spoke a compelling language of its own, which could neither be wholly understood nor in any way ignored. It spoke of darkness and remembered ice, of everlasting winter and a malignant frozen hostility; yet it suggested that terror might not be the last word after all. Here and there, in the configuration of the silent land rising above the blue water, the long bluffs crowned with green unbroken forest, there was the voice of a different spirit.

Go up along the eastern side of Lake Michigan, steer northeast when the land bends away at Point Betsie, and you come before long to Sleeping Bear Point—an incredible flat-topped sand dune rising five hundred feet above the level of the lake and going north for two miles or more. It looks out over the dark water and the islands that lie just offshore, and in the late afternoon the sunlight strikes it and the golden sand turns white, with a pink overlay when the light is just so, and little cloud shadows slide along its face, blue-gray as evening sets in. Sleeping Bear looks eternal, although it is not; this lake took its present shape no more than two or three thousand years ago, and Sleeping Bear is slowly drifting off to the east as the wind shifts its grains of sand, swirling them up one side and dropping them on the other; in a few centuries it will be very different, if indeed it is there at all. Yet if this is a reminder that this part of the earth is still being remodelled, it is also a hint that the spirit back of the remodelling may be worth knowing. In the way this shining dune looks west toward the white storms and the blazing sunsets there is a profound serenity, an unworried affirmation that comes from seeing beyond time and mischance. A woman I know says that to look at the Sleeping Bear late in the day is to feel the same emotion that comes when you listen to Beethoven's *Emperor* Concerto, and she is entirely right. The message is the same. The only trouble is that you have to compose a planet, or great music, to say it persuasively. Beethoven could do it because he was made in the image of God; which suggests that probably there *is* a God, after all.

The men of the Cass expedition, of course, were no mystics, but hardheads who had gone out to count and measure, and to those tasks they devoted themselves. Even so, young Henry Rowe Schoolcraft seems to have been a little touched. Schoolcraft went along as a mineralogist, tapping stones with a hammer and collecting fragments for the Secretary of War, and when he wrote his famous narrative telling what had been seen and done, he was wholly matter-of-fact; too much so, for he had an epic to write, and he composed a War Department report. Yet he seems to have been smitten, somewhere along the way, by a deep feeling for the Indians who lived in this land, and later on he became an Indian agent, established himself at Sault Ste. Marie, and spent most of his time collecting Indian legends and the word-of-mouth tales that passed for Indian history. He got a great tangle of them, and the poet Longfellow eventually read what Schoolcraft wrote down and out of it made the poem *Hiawatha*. This may have been no favor for generations of schoolchildren, who had to read it when they would have preferred to be doing something else, but in a way it was one of the by-products of the odyssey of Lewis Cass.

The men Cass led never lost sight of the fact that their trip into this unknown country would eventually be the means of its transformation. Sooner or later these men in their canoes were going to pull many men after them, and they were well aware of it. The wilderness was to be conquered; this particular bit of earth, craggy and hungry as it might seem, was about to be reshaped, and when the budding scientists in the party made their notes about soils and rocks and plants and temperatures, they were thinking of people who someday would come here

83

to make homes. These later-comers would need to know how to use this country.

That was where the emphasis lay. This country was going to be used; and if this was the case, it was above all things necessary to know about the Indians. Were the British authorities in western Canada in fact inciting them to resist the venturesome Americans—present at that time mostly as fur traders—and if so, how could this be stopped? How many military posts, situated precisely where, would be needed to control the red man and thwart the scheming Briton? Finally, how could the red man be induced to surrender the title to his homeland?

That the Indian's way of life was doomed had been recognized from the very start. President James Monroe had spoken on the subject in a recent message to Congress.

"Independent savage communities," he said, "cannot long exist within the limits of a civilized population. . . . To civilize them, and even to prevent their extinction, it seems to be indispensable that their independence as communities should cease and that the control of the United States over them should be complete and undisputed."

The Secretary of War, John C. Calhoun, who took a much more relaxed view of the proper scope of the authority of the federal government in 1820 than he could take a few years later, had given Cass instructions stressing the importance of working on the Indians so that they would give up their lands to the whites. Calhoun pointed out that speedy settlement of the lower peninsula of Michigan was both inevitable and desirable, and he emphasized the obvious: "This can best be effected by an entire extinguishment of the Indian title."

Entire extinguishment was attained without great delay. Cass had already persuaded the Indians to give up their claim to land around Saginaw Bay. On this trip westward he got title to land on the American side of the St. Marys rapids, and Fort Brady was before long built at Sault Ste. Marie; gifts, oratory, and a subtle reminder that the Americans held all of the high cards seemed to be all that was needed, and in the years that followed Cass's great trip more cessions of title were painlessly negotiated. By 1840, or thereabouts, the Indians had given away the entire state of Michigan. Their independence as communities had ceased, as President Monroe said it should; the Indian's fate was settled, and the wilderness was doomed, windy pine woods, veins of copper-bearing quartz, mountains of iron ore, and all.

As far as the Indian was concerned, the process was relatively humane. A few red men were transplanted bodily to new reservations in the unsettled West, but mostly the Michigan Indians stayed where they were, groping helplessly to grasp the white-man's way, losing their old culture, and finding the new culture hard to assimilate. There were schools and missions here and there to help them, and annual payments from the federal government, and by and large the business was done without the brutality observed in so many other parts of America. After all, these had mostly been friendly Indians.

To be sure, they paid a price. There is a story, probably apocryphal but significant nonetheless, about a United States senator who was running for re-election a few years ago. According to this story, the senator got to a small north-country town one evening, and just before he was led into a hall to make a campaign speech, the local party chairman gave him a briefing about issues that were on people's minds locally.

"You'll notice, at the back of the hall, quite a few Indians," he said. "It would be helpful if somewhere in your speech you could say that you are fully aware of their problem and that you will do your best to solve it."

The senator promised that he would do this. Then—moved by simple curiosity—he asked: "By the way: what is their problem?"

The local man looked at him wide-eyed.

"What's their problem?" he repeated. "God damn it, they're *Indians*!"

Yet the Indian was incidental. It was the land and its great riches that mattered. It passed into American hands just as the tools to exploit it were being perfected—the tools and the driving urge to use them—and the men who held the tools moved in as if they had to get the job finished before nightfall. They succeeded (at any rate, recognizable nightfall has not yet come), and in about a century the job was done. The trees had gone to build homes for half of America, the copper had gone to serve the new age of electricity, and if the iron lasted longer, it had been moved south by millions of tons, in a progress as inexorable as the Sleeping Bear's ponderous drift to the eastward, to make railroads and machinery and skyscrapers and weapons; and the land was left bruised and scarred, with the radar domes to indicate that the age of applied technologies advances with an acceleration that is governed by geometrical progression.

So we live as the Indians of Lewis Cass's time lived, between cultures, compelled to readjust ourselves to forces that will not wait for us. There is no twentieth-century culture; the twentieth century is simply a confused and terrifying time of transition, and the noise of things collapsing is so great that we are taking the prodigious step from the nineteenth century to the twenty-first without a moment of calm in which we can see where we are going. Between nineteenth century and twenty-first there is a gulf as vast as the one the Stone Age Indians had to cross. What's our problem? We're Indians. ☆

Rosa Parks Wouldn't Budge CONTINUED FROM PAGE 64

bama's state and local laws requiring segregation on buses unconstitutional. The Supreme Court acted without listening to any argument; it simply said, "the motion to affirm is granted and the Judgment is affirmed."

Legally, the struggle was over. The black-led and black-supported boycott, rising out of Mrs. Parks's spontaneous act, had resulted in the highest court's driving another nail in the coffin of legalized segregation. But life follows law slowly. It took a month more for the judicial mandate actually to reach Montgomery. In that time the injunction against the car pools was granted. So blacks, still staying off the buses, walked many extra miles when no alternative arrangements were possible.

The interval was used to prepare the black community for the first day of the new dispensation. Sheets of suggestions on how to behave "in a loving manner" were distributed. Role-playing sessions were held in black churches. Among whites reactions varied. The City Commission received front-page coverage to proclaim its "determination [to] do all in its power to oppose the integration of the Negro race with the white race in Montgomery . . . [and] stand like a rock against social equality, intermarriage and mixing of the races under God's creation and plan." But the fateful December 21, the day of official desegregation, came and went with what the Montgomery *Advertiser* called "a calm but cautious acceptance of this significant change in Montgomery's way of life." Black and white ministers sat together undisturbed in what had been the "Whites Only" section. Drivers were uniformly courteous. Most white passengers chose to ignore the innovation; those who made nasty remarks were in turn ignored by the blacks.

There was a swift and violent backlash, a flurry of explosions. On the night of January 9, 1957, four Baptist churches were severely damaged by bombs. Ralph Abernathy's home was virtually destroyed; so was that of Robert Graetz, a young white Lutheran minister who served on the executive board of the M.I.A. A few nights later there was a second at-

The firmness of once-docile blacks riled the die-hards. In Herblock's Washington Post *jibe, one of them cries, "Tote Dat Barge! Lift Dat Boycott! Ride Dat Bus!"*
FROM Herblock's Special For Today (SIMON & SCHUSTER, 1958)

tempt to bomb the King home. A filling station across the street was shattered by an explosion, presumably because its owner had given the F.B.I. the license number of a suspicious car. This tip, however, finally led to the arrest of seven white men who confessed to the January 9 attacks.

Their trial marked the final immediate aftermath of the bus boycott. Their defense attorney, John Blue Hill, was paid from funds collected on Montgomery street corners in plastic buckets bearing the exhortation: SAVE OUR SOUTHERN WAY OF LIFE. His fee was rumored to be five thousand dollars in cash per defendant, and among Montgomeryites a joke circulated that he had stopped the bombings by making it too expensive to continue them. In court he summoned the black boycott leaders to the stand and focussed his questioning on their personal lives and sexual preferences. Most of the testimony was stricken, but not before it made the desired impression on the local all-white—and all-male—jury.

The jury's verdict was rendered with better than deliberate speed, and it was Not Guilty. The bombers left the courtroom with the confident carriage of folk heroes.

Nevertheless, in the long run, their triumph was overshadowed, for at the very moment when the four churches were being attacked, the M.I.A. leadership was in Nashville laying plans for a new organization: the Southern Christian Leadership Conference. Its president was Martin Luther King, Jr.; its basic philosophy was militant nonviolence. Ahead lay many events: sit-ins, freedom rides, gunfire on the campus of the University of Mississippi, the March on Washington, the Civil Rights and Voting Rights acts of 1964 and 1965, the summers of rioting in northern cities—and then, the murder of Martin Luther King, Jr., in a Memphis motel. Perhaps it would take the decade of the seventies to discover the full meaning of the record that began with the Montgomery boycott. But in that January of 1957, as integrated buses rolled down the streets of the Confederacy's first capital, over which the Stars and Bars still flew, almost everyone must have sensed that a new page in the history of black (and white) Americans had been turned.

Janet Stevenson has written an adaptation of the material in this article for young readers. It was recently published in book form by Franklin Watts, Inc., under the title The Montgomery Bus Boycott.

Carpenter-Architects of Key West

CONTINUED FROM PAGE 25

boards, typify the best old houses.

Social considerations aside, wood is a great building material. It is light in proportion to its strength. Unlike concrete, long, unsupported pieces of it will not easily break apart. Any good carpenter who has worked with it can safely judge how thick a piece of lumber should be used for any purpose, even one he has never tried before. He can decide to run his columns up two stories instead of one and pick the dimensions he will then need, without having been trained in the engineering sciences. He does not even have to buy a design manual. Wood is so easy to shape and so simple to connect, unlike steel, that a carpenter-architect with no training beyond his journeyman's experience can relatively easily develop new forms for arches, doorways, rail posts, balustrades. A result of this is a pleasing variety among wooden houses.

In Key West in 1969 more than three hundred houses were still standing that were built in wood before the year 1900; at least one is more than 140 years old. The three hundred houses are concentrated on approximately twenty blocks of the city, immediately surrounding and including its main business street, Duval Street. After the visitor has got used to this sudden plethora of buildings like none he has seen before ("Some of these quaint and charming houses are to be found in no other area in the country," said Robert Garvey, a former executive director of the National Trust for Historic Preservation), he finds that as many as a hundred buildings are distinctive. Of these, twenty-one are included in *Pelican Path*, a guide to Old Key West prepared by the Old Island Restoration Foundation. Five have been meticulously studied by the U.S. government, their dimensions, elevations, plans, and details set down in drawings and notes by the Historical American Buildings Survey of the Department of the Interior. At least twelve others have been noted in the H.A.B.S. records and might have been measured in detail if their owners had not objected to the nuisance and loss of privacy involved in the procedure.

Of the wooden buildings of Key West a few have been saved from demolition by the timely arrival of someone with money and a desire to save the building for its public importance. Captain Geiger's house, in which John James Audubon stayed for several weeks while sketching the birds of the Keys during the 1830's, was saved by Mr. and Mrs. Mitchell Wolfson and turned into a small museum when it was on the brink of disappearance to make way for a filling station. Others have been put to similar adaptive uses as doctors' offices, beauty salons, curiosity shops. But the overwhelming majority of the buildings are still homes for somebody or other. They have not been refurbished en bloc to an agreed-upon standard by wealthy new arrivals or resuscitated by a philanthropic millionaire into a three-dimensional museum, however valuable, in which all animation remains suspended. In Key West one walks past faded house and shiny house, from white house to pink house, from authentic renovation to authentic dilapidation, hearing on Sunday mornings husbands quarrelling with their wives behind the modern jalousies, and observing that while one owner has permitted his saber-sawed gingerbread balustrades to fade and rot untouched, his neighbor, in a misguided fit of neatness, has replaced the original white wooden picket fence with a concrete-block wall washed over with cement grout into which (for ornamentation, one supposes) an occasional terra-cotta tile has been stuck like a square currant in a crust of unbaked dough.

Key West's wooden houses reflect three different periods into which the city's history may conveniently be divided. The Captain Richard Roberts house, one of the two known to have been brought over from the Bahamas by its owner, dates from the earliest period. It was re-erected in Key West in 1847, only twenty-six years after the Senate ratified the purchase of the Territory of Florida from Spain. The change in sovereignty did not extinguish private titles. An Alabama citizen named Simonton purchased the uninhabited island of Key West from its Spanish owner in 1821 for two thousand dollars and promptly sold off three-quarters of his purchase to others. Within a few months settlers began to arrive; the most permanent was the United States Navy, which, after hearing the report of a survey party, established a naval station under the command of Commodore David Porter, remembered for sturdy service in controlling piracy in Caribbean waters. The Navy has had a permanent installation at Key West ever since, but its size and importance have changed over the years, with corresponding effect on the economic health of the civilian city.

The civilian settlers who began to arrive at Key West were also interested in the location of the island with respect to shipping in the Caribbean area. Their interest was not strategic, however. More menacing to the Caribbean trade than Porter's naval guns were the persistent east winds of the south Florida coast and the long, treacherous, and unmarked Florida Strait. The earliest Key West settlers were seafaring men from New England and elsewhere who saw the financial possibilities in salvage. Sometimes they themselves had been shipwrecked on the Florida reef and salvaged by a Key West wrecker. The rule of the sea awards the first captain at the scene of a wreck the special status of wrecking master: he is entitled to a special share of the fee payable for saving the vessel or its cargo, or both. From the tops of houses in Key West the wreckers could keep an eye on a long section of the reef, dashing down to their salvage sloops at a sign that someone was in trouble, in much the same way that a modern automobile wrecker keeps his short-wave radio tuned to police frequencies in the hope of hearing about new business. Other captains cruised the reef in search of someone needing help.

Key West was a wrecker's paradise. The climate was equable, and there were plenty of potential customers. Thirty American vessels cleared Havana each week; twenty more cleared the smaller port of Matanzas on the north coast of Cuba. To go home with their cargoes of sugar and rum they had to sail past Key West, only eighty miles from Havana, and keep to the strait between the Florida reef and the Bahamas. If only a fraction of these ships were wrecked on the reef and only a small portion of the value of the cargo paid to the wreckers for salvage, there was still a handsome sum of money to be divided among the wreckers of Key West. Business in the city expanded.

Once a disabled ship had been pulled off a reef or its cargo unloaded —often at great risk—outside assistance was necessary to decide on the value and necessity of the wreckers' services. Before Florida's status was settled by international treaty with Great Britain, the salvaged cargo and the salvaged vessels were taken to the Bahamas for adjudication of a proper fee, and usually for auction of the goods saved in order to raise the amount. Simonton, no doubt still interested in the prosperity of his investment in Key West real estate, wrote to the House of Representatives in 1828 pointing out that the government was losing the revenue from court fees and duty on the goods sold by permitting vessels wrecked in American territorial waters to be taken elsewhere for the adjudication of salvage. In response the Congress passed a law requiring that all vessels wrecked in American waters be brought to the nearest American port, and to take care of wrecks in the Florida Strait the government established a court at Key West.

An immediate result of the new law was a drop in the wrecking business in the Bahamas, whereupon a number of outstanding Bahamian wrecking captains moved to Key West and became American residents and ultimately American citizens. Captain Richard Roberts was one such. He came over in 1847, bringing his disassembled house with him, probably because the hurricane of 1846 had destroyed many of Key West's homes and it was then difficult to find builders and materials for new ones.

The Roberts house, which is still standing and in use, is a splendid example of simple conch architecture, designed to provide sturdy protection against hurricanes and having long, shady porches. To conserve interior space the stairs to the second floor are on the outside of the house; the stairs to the third floor are more like a companionway in a ship than a flight inside a house. The landing at the top of this nearly vertical flight is so narrow it suggests a crow's nest; one must maneuver around the banisters sideways to get to the two rooms on the top floor, one at each side of the stairs. The rooms are ventilated by hatches cut into the roof.

"Significant architectural features," says the Historical American Buildings Survey in discussing the Roberts house, "include porches along the long dimensions of the house at both floor levels, exterior stairway, wide beaded-edge siding and mortise and tenon joinery." The present resident of the house, who has survived three Key West hurricanes, describes the house as "riding with the storms." The interior walls and ceilings are made of boards as wide as eighteen inches; there is no plaster in the house.

Captain Roberts, according to local historians, was a southern sympathizer during the Civil War, as were many other Key Westers, including particularly those who arrived from the Bahamas after the abolition of slavery there. Since Key West remained firmly in Union hands throughout the entire war, the captain moved up the west coast of Florida and operated a blockade-runner. He returned to Key West after the war and, having married three times, produced enough Roberts offspring to confuse local genealogists and cataloguers of Key West houses. His youngest daughter by his third wife continued to live in the Roberts house until 1964.

The wrecking business that was supposed to provide Key West with perpetual prosperity flourished until the Civil War, reaching a high point of 2.8 million dollars in 1855.

But gradually it began to taper off. Lighthouses were built to mark the Florida reef (over the opposition of Key Westers, some said), and marine safety's gain became the salvage business' loss. But the final blow was the development of steam navigation. Having broken their dependence on the wind, shipmasters made the passage through the Florida Strait with so few accidents that the wrecking fleet could no longer depend on salvage fees to stay alive.

The incipient depression that resulted was cured by several new industries—sponge fishing (until it was killed by a sponge blight), shipping and ship chandlery generally, and, most important, a number of activities that flourished on a political if not a coral reef: Cuban unrest. Success in these circumstances required somewhat more sophistication than the rough-and-ready atmosphere of the wrecking days. The John Lowe, Jr., house, recorded in detail by the Historical American Buildings Survey in 1967, is typical of this second period.

John Lowe, Jr., who built the house from a load of lumber that he brought in himself from Pensacola, was a generation younger than Captain Roberts of the Roberts house. Lowe was born in Key West of parents who had emigrated from the Bahamas. He earned his shipmaster's license at the age of thirteen but chose to spend his life ashore clerking in the mercantile business established by a brother-in-law, William Curry. He later went into business for himself, owning a fleet of sponge vessels and trading schooners. The house indicates he prospered.

At a casual glance Lowe's appears to be a white wooden house very like the Roberts house and unmistakably a Key West house. But the differences are remarkable. While the Roberts house seems to have been built with portability in mind, rather like a mobile home, the John Lowe, Jr., house is grand in conception and imposing in dimension. The ceiling heights in the Roberts house suggest the tautness of shipboard space; in the Lowe house the ground-floor ceilings are twelve feet high; the living room is thirty feet long; spacious porches surround the main body of the house on three sides; and a fine staircase rises from the central hallway into which the front door opens. On the left of the main central hallway is a study, and behind it a fine classic dining room. Upstairs, at the second-floor level, a second porch runs across the front and sides of the house punctuated by the slim, square white columns that extend all the way to the roof line. The roof slants straight down from the ridge of the house to the columns at the outside edge of the second-floor balcony. "The Captain John Lowe, Jr., house is typical of mid-19th century homes built by successful mariners of Key West," H.A.B.S. tells us. "Its design was influenced by a classic revival, island architecture and shipbuilding techniques evident in its proportions, trim and construction."

On the top of the roof stands a broad widow's walk from which one gets a fine view of all of the island of Key West and its harbor. The widow's walk was originally an enclosed cupola. It blew off in a hurricane in 1919; discretion seems to have dictated its replacement by the open walk: the wind can whistle harmlessly between the balusters.

Three years after the Civil War a new set of episodes started in Spain that made possible Key West's most spectacular wave of prosperity. The original event was simply a short-

John James Audubon shed unexpected immortality upon John Geiger's house, far left, by staying there while painting tropic birds in the 1830's. Below is the oldest house in Key West, a rugged survivor of hurricanes and history since 1825. The John Lowe, Jr., house, right center, had verandahs and a widow's walk; it is the same house depicted by Mario Sanchez on page 24. Captain Richard Roberts brought his house, far right, piecemeal from the Bahamas.

lived 1868 Spanish republican uprising. Cubans expected that the new regime would permit Cuba, a colony, far more self-government than she had previously enjoyed. When this happy hope failed to materialize, some Cubans began a revolutionary movement that became a ten-year war.

There is a general sense in the world that no good will come to you if your livelihood depends on other people's misfortunes, but this did not prove true for Key West. First it had thrived on wrecking; now it profited from the agony of Cuba's history. In that island's struggles Key West was beneficiary and stimulant. When Cubans and their American friends tried to assist the revolutionary forces in the Civil War of 1868–78, Key West was the principal base. When fighting broke out again in 1895 and American journalists tried to write dispatches on Cuban atrocities for a public hungry to be shocked, Key West provided the cable office through which the dispatches came. When Cubans fled their country, either temporarily while preparing what they thought would be its liberation or permanently as exiles, Key West, more than any other city, attracted them and prospered by their skills.

Key West was centrally involved in 1873 in the first serious international incident arising from the efforts of filibusters—private armies of exiles and adventurers—to free Cuba. This was the case of the *Virginius*, an American-flag steam-powered commercial vessel. Its commander was Captain Joseph Fry, a New Orleans man who had lived in Key West as a child. The *Virginius* was allegedly a gunrunner or a transport for mercenary revolutionaries. Ignoring the U.S. flag and non-Spanish nationality of the majority of the men on board, Cuban colonial officials, quite without valid international precedent, pursued her into Jamaican waters, captured her, and brought her back to Santiago. There, over the protests of the American and British consuls, the local governor declared the ship a pirate and began to execute its officers and crew, killing fifty-two of them before the arrival of a British warship put a stop to the massacre. American newspapers screamed for revenge, and President Grant was persuaded to demand an apology and reparations. To back his threats he assembled the North Atlantic fleet, consisting of obsolete and deteriorated equipment left over from the Civil War. Key West, of course, was the closest port to Cuba, and the fleet limped there, with some of the older vessels, particularly the ironclads, scarcely able to make their way down the coast. Ultimately, the Spanish, perhaps moved by this threat, agreed to give back the *Virginius*—not much of a prize in herself, since she could not make it back to Key West under her own steam. The whole unsatisfying affair, however, threw Key West into prominence as the port most likely to provide a threat to Spain in Cuba and to provide a haven for Cuban refugees.

They soon came in droves, bringing an industry with them. Already, Francisco Marrero, a Cuban who had been arrested in nearby Havana in 1869 on a charge of treason and imprisoned there, had won his release and come to Key West. He opened a cigar factory on Front Street in Key West; many more such businesses followed his. By the middle of the decade of the seventies there were twenty-nine cigar factories in Key West, employing, according to an 1876 count, nearly 2,100 people. In the 1880's the number rose even higher. Naturally, the growth of the cigar business and its employment brought revenues into the city that in turn sustained a demand for other goods. In 1874 more American vessels entered Key West than entered Charleston, Savannah, Mobile, and St. Johns, Florida, combined, a statistic somewhat lessened in impressiveness by the fact that unlike those cities, Key West could not be reached at all by land.

The cigar factories provided more than employment for the Cubans. They provided gathering places where support for revolutionary activities could be mobilized. A revolutionary junta in New York City coordinated such undertakings. Its mainspring was José Martí, a writer and orator jailed by the authorities in 1868 at the age of sixteen and thereafter, during a short lifetime, dedicated to freeing Cuba. It was he who was primarily responsible for organizing work among Cuban exiles in Key West and Tampa. Martí was killed in 1895 on a revolutionary expedition. But disorganized and sometimes totally disconnected efforts at armed filibustering against the Spanish regime in Cuba persisted. Key West was of peculiar importance in all of these paramilitary ventures, because it supplied either the funds or the vessels or the equipment or, best of all, a haven for retreat when the filibusterers were chased out of Cuban waters by Spanish warships. Key West was the port of refuge, for example, to which Napoleon Bonaparte Broward—later to become governor of Florida—brought his tugboat, *The Three Friends*, after a comparatively successful expedition in March, 1896, during which he claimed to have put ashore in Cuba some sixty-five men with a modest quantity of arms.

It cannot be claimed that providing a base of operations for filibusterers was an important source of revenue to the citizens of Key West in the eighties or nineties, but it was a valuable demonstration of the importance of effective municipal publicity. The cable to Havana, laid in 1867, made Key West the natural center of news from that island; and any rumors passing through Key West, even if they originated no closer to Cuba than the cigar factories on Duval Street, carried a measure of plausibility. There is some evidence also that the illicit gun-and-soldier trade—like the rum-running trade that came thirty years later—kept busy some of the vessels that otherwise might have lain idle.

The mariner who has lost a boat is from a Key West monument to the Maine's *victims.*
BROWN BROS.

In any case Key West's participation in the episode of Spanish, Cuban, and American affairs reached its climax during the Spanish-American War. As the telegraph station nearest to Cuba, it was the place where correspondents hurried, on private yachts chartered by newspapers, to file their dispatches—a practice that had been initiated before the war's actual outbreak in order to avoid the Spanish censors in Havana.

During the war itself, limited land access to Key West meant that Jacksonville and Tampa served as more important ports of embarkation for the Army, but the port of Key West was still important for naval supplies and fuel.

The booming conditions produced by all these events caused a tremendous demand for new housing. The third major period of Key West carpenter architecture began in the seventies and was now supplemented by the construction of several important public buildings, including a convent and a handsome brick post office. The latter, built in the nineties, was later acquired by the Navy and is still used as part of the naval base. Over the years the Navy, while maintaining the building meticulously, has managed to add a few false and discordant accents, closing in open porches, tinkering with the roof line, and inserting jangly aluminum sashes in the Richardsonlike window openings. The building remains a vigorous and strong example of its style and has been recorded in detail by H.A.B.S.

The eighties and nineties were the period in Key West in which the Gothic Revival went south. The buildings erected then, though they retained many of the same qualities of basic simplicity and clean line that distinguished their predecessors, added so much ornamentation in the way of fretted wood balustrades, corner brackets at the porch column heads, and even stand-up wooden icing along the roof ridges, that many visitors to Key West form the instant impression that the lacework is the essential, intrinsic feature of Key West architecture.

The Historical American Buildings Survey has noted some thirty different patterns of balustrades used in Key West at the height of the Gothic Revival. These range from fairly simple elementary cutouts in which two adjacent diamonds meet at their broadest point while at the rail line and the foot of the banister the apexes flourish in a scalloped semiround, to far more elaborate designs with heart-shaped cutouts, and others too involved even to attempt to describe. These designs, according to local legend, were developed to their romantic high point by a Cuban Negro craftsman named Francisco Camello, who operated a wood-carving plant in Key West in the eighties. Nowadays if one is faced with replacing any of the balustrades, he can consult Howard Englund, a civilian architect attached to the public works department of the naval base. Englund has made templates of each of the designs, and local millwork establishments can reproduce the designs from his templates. None of this helps with the really elaborate ornamentation, however. Some of these include lathe-turned wooden spokes inserted in wooden arcs or crossed with each other in the kind of complex intertwining that suggests filigree jewelry. These designs are often used in conjunction with turned wooden columns, which are standard in a number of Gothic adaptations of the basic Key West style.

In the 1930's, when the whole Victorian epoch was reviled generally by the makers of taste in America, the structures of Key West's third period were rather contemptuously regarded. A writer for the WPA, in an unsigned unpublished manuscript at the P. K. Yonge Library of Florida History of the University of Florida, refers to the "varied yet fussy and monotonous decorative elements" of the Gothic Revival, but even the nameless critic admitted a feeling for the interior wood curtains and the ceiling murals that are sometimes found in the more extravagant examples. Today, as the functional criteria of architectural beauty that seemed so important in the thirties are close to realization, the ornamentation of the Victorian period has come back into style, a welcome relief from bad Bauhaus; and many find appeal in the exuberance, confidence, and even the extravagance and perhaps the unsophistication that marked Key West's third architectural period.

But long before mid-twentieth-century critics appraised Key West's "Gothic period," the prosperity that had produced it stopped. The cigar business moved to Tampa, perhaps because of labor difficulties compounded by the political complications of the Cuban-Spanish rivalry; perhaps simply because rail and road transportation was better from Tampa. When this industry left, it was, unlike salvaging, replaced by nothing. When the Spanish-American War ended and the Panama Canal was built, Guantánamo Bay on the south coast of Cuba, not Key West, became the Gibraltar of the Caribbean. The naval base dwindled instead of growing. In 1912 a new day seemed possible when the wildest of all Floridian schemes, the construction of the Florida East Coast Railway—120 miles over the Keys from Florida City to Key West—was completed, but it had no economic significance whatsoever. Its owner, Henry M. Flagler, made some pretense of believing the railroad would thrive by carrying sport fishermen to Key West and bringing back goods, but fundamentally the line was his toy, built by a personal investment of fifty million dollars in the spirit of an Oriental prince constructing the Taj Mahal. It did nothing to check Key West's decline.

In 1935 one of the most disastrous hurricanes ever to hit the Keys destroyed and undermined so much of the railroad line that no one wanted to rebuild it. For three years the island was once again cut off from dry connection with mainland Florida; but federal funds came to the rescue, and the roadbed was converted into a two-lane highway. This road, as it turned out, did revive Key West. Carrying not the sport fishermen foreseen by Flagler, but simpler Americans made mobile with trailers and outboard motorboats, it has put the Keys—including Key West—within the range of middle-class America in an age of postwar affluence and leisure. Some of these visitors are carrying out vows to make the pleasant town their retirement home. In addition, from the start of World War II the naval base, down to a complement of fourteen men in 1932, stirred with new life, not so much because of its strategic location but because its warm surrounding water provided a fine testing and training ground for underwater weapons and personnel. And finally, a shrimp fleet based in Key West and fishing throughout the Gulf of Mexico now employs— on the boats and ashore—as many people as once rolled cigars and gave dimes to Martí and his junta.

The potential new boom may make or break Key West's heritage. Perhaps, drawn to the palm-fronded patios and the honest craft of the carpenter-architects, enough wealthy Americans will buy and maintain the old buildings of Key West to save the national treasure they constitute. Perhaps, instead, these homes will fall before the great need for efficient concrete-block retirement homes on the island acreage of this small but climatically blessed island, and the creations of the old-time master workmen will simply continue to disappear, little by little, a building at a time, until as little is left of them as was of the wrecking masters, the sponge divers, and the New York journalists sitting in a vanished telegraph office and spinning tales of atrocities that helped to send two nations off to war.

Roger Starr, a housing and urban affairs specialist, wrote "This Is The Way the World Ends" in AMERICAN HERITAGE, *October, 1970.*

The Drought and the Dole

CONTINUED FROM PAGE 19

worried because the 1930 crop of infants seemed less sturdy than usual. They attributed it to undernourishment caused by the drought and heat. That fall Malcolm Cowley of the *New Republic* drove south from New York to Tennessee. Rich vistas had turned into wasteland, and handbills advertised farms for sale at auction. "Everywhere," he reported, "the fields were the color of old straw matting. The weeds in the fencerows, even, had shriveled like rose leaves in an old album. . . . In Tennessee, the rains had come in time to save most of the tobacco crop, but the corn was ruined and there would be no hay to carry the stock through the winter." Cows nibbled on grass roots or milled around dwindling strawstacks ordinarily used only for bedding; often their ribs showed.

It became increasingly obvious that Hoover's program was not working. His pleas had failed to dislodge loan money from private sources; rural bankers were already too deeply in trouble to extend more credit. Announcing public works was one thing; actually starting them was another, and they ordinarily conformed to plans made years before. New roads rarely seemed to run through areas where the drought was worst, and even when they did, contractors were reluctant to hire unskilled farmers. (That probably explained the trouble in Lonoke County.) Railroad rate reductions did some good, but they lasted only until October 1; the real feed crisis would come in the winter months. Drought victims looked to the Red Cross as their best hope, only to find, in the words of one high official, that the agency regarded it as "psychologically unsound" to intervene until local authorities could no longer cope.

Casting a weather eye toward the months ahead, the assistant director for Red Cross relief in the Midwest estimated shortly after the White House conference that "in some counties there will be a few dozen families and [in] others perhaps 100 or 200 families that will need food provided by some agency next winter. Thousands of families, of course, will need to skimp." By the end of 1930 the Red Cross had in fact provided food and clothing to 50,000 families, at a cost of $500,000. That was an average of $10 per family, a drop in an empty bucket and hardly a dent in the original $5,000,000 pledge. But money, and a great deal of it, was needed as badly as rain now. Harris Gaylord Warren, one of Hoover's few reliable—and sympathetic—biographers, has put that need at $85,000,000 in loans for 330,000 farm families in the fifteen states hardest hit. To the balancer of the budget, the figure was appalling; to the desperate man on the receiving end, it could mean the two or three hundred dollars that would carry him through the winter.

Late in November, just before the three-month lame-duck session of the outgoing 71st Congress opened, Red Cross officials, congressional leaders, and other interested parties met to discuss the drought situation. This conference, held at the Department of Agriculture, agreed to back loans for seed, fertilizer, tractor fuel, feed for animals, and—despite the predictable administration murmurings about the dole—loans for food relief. The estimated appropriation was $60,000,000, and there were tentative indications that the President would support it. But the administration proceeded to introduce an alternative measure, which asked for only $25,000,000 and which pointedly excluded food loans. To many, particularly those senators and congressmen from the drought states, the administration package was noth-

Hoover also favored private charity as the means of feeding hungry urbanites. Here, in a carefully posed picture taken in December, 1932, Mrs. Hoover, left, presents a bulging food basket to a grateful elderly woman at Salvation Army headquarters in Washington.

ing more than another instance of the notoriously poor liaison between the White House and Capitol Hill. They treated it as an outright double-cross.

The President's reasons were plain, but in this case words spoke louder than actions. At a press conference late in December, Hoover declared that if all the bills, "mostly in the guise of giving relief," were lumped together, they would cost four and a half billion dollars above his budgetary recommendations. "Prosperity cannot be restored by raids on the treasury," he said, adding with a touch of self-righteousness that he refused to play politics "at the expense of human misery." His tormentors would not forget that unhappy phrase.

What the public did not know was that Hoover had finally tried to start a great voluntary drive for drought and unemployment relief comparable to his European efforts. But leaders of local relief programs had balked, expressing the fear that their own money-raising campaigns would be doomed by such a drive; Hoover's visionary project died, unrecognized and unmourned. It was yet another splendid opportunity missed. From administration sources there came only the predictable invocation of the spectre of the dole: food relief, even in the form of loans, was perilously close to being one. Just before the Christmas recess Congress reached a compromise and agreed on a $45,000,000 loan appropriation for feed, seed, and the like, with the food provision left out. The matter seemed closed, though an undeniable residue of doubt and bad feelings lingered. As Joseph T. Robinson, of Arkansas, the Democratic minority leader in the Senate, commented during the debate, "It is all right to put a mule on the dole, but it is condemned, I see, to put a man on a parity with a mule."

The *dole*. That overpowering, all-encompassing word of illusion in the Hoover years. It was charged with the same amorphous malignity and colored with the same sickly foreign taint as the word *Red* in 1919. And in the same way, the word as Americans used it bore little relation to the real thing. The dole in Great Britain had originated in the early part of the century as an unemployment insurance scheme, to which workers, employers, and the state all contributed. But under the pressure of a seemingly unshakable postwar depression, it had begun to assume the character of straight poor relief. The publicists of America's New Era delighted in spreading pictures of the gaunt people "on the dole" sitting hopelessly in bare, airless kitchens made more ghastly by the illumination of photographer's flash powder, or queuing up in some soot-blackened Midlands street with its changeless horizon of slate roofs and cannon-mouthed chimney pots, the industrial revolution gone in the teeth. Whether they were the stunted children or the prematurely aged girls of Wigan and Manchester, their attitude was invariably one of supine waiting: "The soul-destroying dole" was a bit of catching euphony coined by a group of Boston bankers during that winter. To Americans it appeared as though the dole had caused the depression in England, and not the other way round.

A government handout, be it shillings or a few dollars, would strip a person of his self-reliance and his pride in his own accomplishments; it would create a situation in which he ceased to feel guilt for living by the sweat of someone else's brow—so this line of reasoning went. The dole was not only against our traditions but would end by wrecking them. The word, as intimation or accusation, could be a potent political weapon, and even progressives like Governor Franklin D. Roosevelt of New York shielded themselves with *pro forma* declarations against it.

In the conservative view the dole had come to mean any sort of direct federal aid to an individual. Once the government established a precedent by giving food relief to hungry farmers in the drought states, where could it draw the line? Next the unemployed in the cities would be clamoring for the same treatment. Hoover did not want to commit himself to what he believed to be an irrevocable step. Like his hero Woodrow Wilson, he worried about his historical role quite as much as his day-to-day administrative one: ideal was as important as action, and a fine balance had to be maintained between the two. He was convinced that nothing less than the soul of America, along with everything the New Era stood for, was at stake—and so, perhaps, he tended to credit the most optimistic things his in-

From the doorway of their miserable shack an Arkansas sharecropper and his family welcome a Red Cross worker around 1930.
LIBRARY OF CONGRESS

formants told him about the health of the nation.

Since cancelling his western vacation Hoover had taken only three brief excursions out of the Washington area, to deliver speeches in the congressional campaign of 1930. It is hard to say whether the Democrats would have registered such impressive gains if he had made himself more conspicuous; but it seems clear that in the strenuous isolation of the White House—has a President ever worked so hard?—he was out of touch with much of the discontent and genuine desperation of the country. This was nowhere more evident than in his handling of the drought.

Hoover was playing for time. The prevailing assumption was that once the nation got through the winter, the worst would be past. The administration seized on every favorable twitch of the expiring economy as a sign of inevitable upswing. Spring would bring one as surely as it would bring rain, and the principle of voluntary aid would have withstood the onslaughts of all dole-like compromises. The result would vindicate Hoover's Presidential leadership—that, too, was important if he hoped to reverse the trend of depression. But Hoover had obviously failed to allow for the consquences of a chance boiling over, and right after New Year's one occurred which reopened the question of drought relief in the most painful and damaging way.

It is not impossible that Herbert Hoover's career in the White House turned on the accidental inspiration of a tenant farmer in Arkansas. His name was H. C. Coney, and he was one of those ordinarily anonymous persons who, without meaning to, sometimes leave a permanent mark on their time. The 1930's seemed made for his kind, which was a measure of how far events had run beyond the control of the men who were supposed to control them. What many Americans at the beginning of 1931 feared that somebody would do, Coney did. They were lucky that he was a good man who never stepped out of character, who asked only for what he needed and did not reach for more. As a model for a hero of proletarian fiction he is a bust. We do not find him crying out to his oppressed fellows at the end, "We gotta make a union!" and with a linking of arms and a shouldering of rifles, marching forward to solidarity. Even so, the repercussions of his small attempt to make things better would haunt and discredit Hoover's grand strategy for fighting the Depression. From this point on in his administration, the President would remain on the defensive, caricatured as a hardhearted bungler in a stiff collar by his political opponents and, gradually, by much of the public that had once revered him.

H. C. Coney worked forty-one acres of cotton land near the town of England—appropriate name—in Lonoke County. He was forty-six years old, married, and the father of five sons; tuberculosis in his boyhood

In the cities, destitute men made a few pennies selling apples on street corners. A 1931 cartoon by Daniel Fitzpatrick is titled "The Farmer Joins the Apple Vendor."

had partially crippled him. All his life he had been a renter. "I have tried to get able to buy me a home," he later related, "but about the time I thought I was about to reach the goal, along came 1930 and buried me alive." Coney had been hit hard by the drought, but he was better off than some: at least his family was not starving.

Then, on January 3, a Saturday, a woman neighbor came to his place and told him that her children hadn't eaten for two days. She was crying. As Coney put it, something went up in his head. He asked her to wait while he and his wife drove over in his truck to the Red Cross depot. He found a crowd of men already gathered there. They were pleading with the Red Cross agent, who refused to give them food because his supply of application blanks for relief had run out. Others, men who had been relatively prosperous until the disaster of the summer, were being turned away because they were too warmly dressed; the Red Cross was obsessed with the fear of "impostors."

Coney shouted to them to climb on: they would get food in England if they had to take it. Forty-odd men accompanied him, clinging to his old truck as it puttered, a little more sullenly than usual, toward the main street. Newspaper accounts alleged that some were carrying guns. Though Coney and other eyewitnesses later denied it—and the spontaneous character of the demonstration would seem to make the possibility unlikely—the guns were the detail that stuck in people's minds. Were things really *this* bad? Was somebody hiding the truth?

Coney and his small party first sought out the mayor and the police chief. By this time a sizable crowd had collected, and it soon became apparent that there were many others desperate for food. A local lawyer named George Morris tried to calm the gathering. He was interrupted by shouts: "We are not going to let our children starve." "We want food and we want it now." Meanwhile merchants made panicky calls to Red Cross regional offices in Little Rock and St. Louis. The St. Louis authorities suggested that they issue $2.75 worth of food for each family but hedged about reimbursement: food orders could not be approved unless they were made on the regulation application blanks. The Red Cross promised to rush a fresh supply. The England merchants, many of whom were broke themselves, finally decided that it was better to distribute free food than to risk being looted. By late evening, from three to five hundred persons had been provided with food. As Morris said, "These men and women who came here today just simply got hungry, that's all. Why, one man told me they were impostors, but when I saw those women standing before me, crying openly and begging food for their children, they can't tell me they are impostors."

There had been "bread riots" in the cities before this, but they could be, and usually were (with good reason) dismissed as Communist publicity stunts. But H. C. Coney and his kind could not be branded with any of the customary epithets of political opprobrium—though some of Hoover's well-intentioned supporters tried to do so. Here were white, American-born farmers, not foreign Reds from a ghetto, behaving like revolutionaries. "Paul Revere just woke up Concord, these birds woke up America," Will Rogers wrote in his boxed "letter" syndicated to newspapers from coast to coast. He went on to warn: ". . . you let this country get hungry and they are going to eat, no matter what happens to Budgets, Income Taxes or Wall Street values. Washington mustn't forget who rules when it comes to a show down."

But Washington gave every sign of having forgotten. The President refused to believe what had happened in England, terming it in his *Memoirs* an "alleged riot by 'starving people.' . . . When I sent my military aide, Colonel Hodges, to investigate the 'riot' [which Hoover placed in February], he found that it was a fake." The demonstration hadn't been a riot, of course, but Hoover had missed the point. In fairness to him, however, it should be pointed out that the drought had not produced a famine comparable to the Russian one in the early 1920's, when his re-

Sympathy for the Depression's victims was not unanimous. A 1931 cartoon shows Mr. Average Citizen, feet by a cozy fire, brooding about the loss of American self-reliance.

lief efforts (largely depending on federally appropriated money) had saved an estimated ten million lives. Perhaps that memory clouded his view. It was one of those needless ironies of history that Herbert Hoover, the man who had gained his fame by feeding the hungry of the world, should have been undone by his apparent insensitivity to starvation at home.

The reaction of the administration to the England incident was as sluggish as it was surly and did little to calm the increasingly uneasy feelings of the public. England was just twenty miles from Little Rock, and reporters must have rushed to the town that afternoon. The story, as told by the Associated Press and others, became nationwide news. Next morning, readers of the *New York Times* found an account on the front page of the Sunday edition, and the governor of Arkansas, Harvey Parnell, felt it necessary to wire the paper that conditions "are by no means alarming and no rioting or violence in any form has taken place. . . ." Pointing to the demonstration, Left-leaning journals such as the *New Republic* and the *Nation* hastened to reassure subscribers that the Depression was worse than anyone imagined. And the influential *Arkansas Gazette* of Little Rock agonized over the "unfortunate" publicity that England had brought the state.

Three days after H. C. Coney had led his band of farmers to the England grocery store—put that way, the whole affair seems so tiny—the Senate voted to add $15,000,000 for food loans to the drought-relief bill. In the House, where unanimous consent was needed to send the original $45,000,000 measure into a House-Senate conference for final modifications, Congressman Fiorello La Guardia of New York stood up and announced that he would withhold his support until the unemployed in the cities were granted a food loan equal to the Senate proposal for drought victims. La Guardia kept up his lonely fight for three days, long enough to make his point—and to confirm Hoover's worst fears.

Meanwhile the chairman of the Red Cross, John Barton Payne, appeared before the Senate Appropriations Committee. Judge Payne, a wealthy Virginian who had been Wilson's last Secretary of the Interior, claimed some expertise on the drought matter: seventy-six acres of corn land on his Piedmont estate had failed to yield a single bushel in the summer of 1930. Payne thought that the $4,500,000 remaining in his

PAGE 94: IN THE ST. LOUIS *Post-Dispatch*; PAGE 95: JOHN T. MCCUTCHEON, 1931, REPRINTED COURTESY OF THE CHICAGO *Tribune* agency's special fund for drought relief was probably sufficient for the winter: "I do not say that we can get through on four and one-half millions, but I say if we get toward the bottom of the barrel, we will yell." Less than a week later Payne was making noises that sounded suspiciously like a yell. On January 10 he asked for, and got, Hoover's approval for a $10,000,000 public appeal to aid farmers stricken by the drought.

That seemed to settle the matter—or did it? Though the House finally rejected the $15,000,000 food-loan bill, the Senate had not exhausted its capacity for making mischief at the expense of the President. Senator Joseph T. Robinson of Arkansas, who himself came from Lonoke County, now proposed to offer the Red Cross an outright gift of $25,000,000 for food and medicine for sick and hungry farmers and—in deference to city congressmen like La Guardia—for the unemployed. Payne did not overwhelm his potential benefactors with gratitude. "All I pray for is for Congress to let us alone," he announced, without bothering to hide his irritation. "If we can't do the job, then let Congress kick us." He also blamed the Robinson bill for an early lag in contributions. The Senate voted the money anyway.

Even administration stalwarts showed signs of weakening at this point; one compromise proposal would have had the government giving the $25,000,000 to the Red Cross —as a loan. By Hooverian logic, that would simply have put the Red Cross on the dole. Payne announced that he would refuse the grant, and the President intimated that he would veto it; the House, loaded with conservative holdovers from the 1928 election, proceeded to kill the Robinson bill. The victory was Hoover's, but the cost may not have been worth it. His opponents vied with one another in a frolic of sarcasm. "The best way to feed the unemployed would be to move them to China and Russia," said Senator Alben Barkley of Kentucky, in a pointed reference to Hoover's international relief projects and the government's financial role in them. Senator George W. Norris of Nebraska resorted to beatitudes: "Blessed be they who starve while the asses and mules are fed, for they shall be buried at public expense."

Congress dithered, the Red Cross drive sputtered along, and starving people in the drought regions got little to eat in the process. Something was wrong; the well of charity appeared to have dried up, too. Maybe there had been too many appeals of late; maybe Americans were holding on to their extra dimes and dollar bills. Judge Payne and the President mounted a tremendous publicity operation. Business leaders like Owen D. Young of General Electric and the power magnate Samuel Insull—he was still mightily solvent, as far as the world knew— were enlisted, as were entertainment figures like Amos 'n Andy and Will Rogers. Rogers visited Hoover at the White House before flying west to raise money. "Had a long talk with our President this morning," he reported in his letter of January 16. "He sincerely feels (with almost emotion) that it would set a bad precedent for the Government to appropriate money for the Red Cross. He feels that once the Government relieves the people, they will always expect it. . . ."

Rogers obviously had his doubts, but he was ready to help in spite of them. From Little Rock, on the evening of the twenty-second, the cowboy humorist presided over a nationwide radio appeal featuring the voices of the President, Calvin Coolidge, Al Smith, and Mary Pickford. Nine thousand watched him in Wichita Falls, Texas, eighteen thousand in Forth Worth. Passing through Fort Smith, Arkansas, in February, he noted a touching bit of Depressionana: a small circus had been stranded there, totally busted, and the town was keeping it alive—elephants, tigers, and performers alike. "Well folks, sure glad to be here with you, glad you are starving, otherwise I would never have met you," Rogers's warm-up patter began.

You have nothing on the rest of the country. We are all starving. We haven't had a regular meal since the Democrats were in, and if we wait for em to get back in again we may never get another one. . . . Starving ain't so bad, it's getting used to it that is tough. The first three years of a Republican Administration is the hardest. By the end of that time you are used to living on predictions. . . .

His audiences loved these mordant fillips; by the end of his tour he had collected $225,000 for drought relief, or almost half of what the Red Cross had spent the previous autumn.

The papers dutifully recorded other notable donations. J. P. Morgan gave $50,000. John D. Rockefeller, Jr., $250,000. Thomas A. Edison donated his eighty-third, and last, birthday cake to the Red Cross, which auctioned it off for $107. Convicts in the Tennessee State Penitentiary sent in $51, while a thief presented a stolen stock certificate, which the Red Cross magnanimously returned to its rightful owner; it probably wasn't worth much anyway. But the appeal soon lost what small momentum it had. By February 1 less than half of the fund had been collected; the $10,000,000 goal was not passed until mid-March, two months after the drive had been initiated. The winter was all but over then, and many regarded the lagging gifts as an indication of how inadequate private relief was in dealing quickly with emergencies of this size.

That, along with the unabated uproar in Congress and the country, finally pushed the administration toward compromise. The Senate was threatening to force an extra session, and there was no telling what trouble might result. Hoover, palpably stung by the fury of his attackers, tried to defend his actions in a public statement issued on February 3. The document was full of the affronted stiffness and bland defiance of his recent Presidential utterances—why did Hoover, who was never facile with the language, always insist on writing his own speeches? And yet, a hint of sadness and bewilderment ran through it:

I have indeed spent much of my life in fighting hardship and starvation both abroad and in the Southern states. I do not feel that I should be charged with lack of human sympathy for those who suffer.... I am proud to have sought the help of Congress in the past for nations who were so disorganized by war and anarchy that self-help was impossible. ... There is no such paralysis in the United States....

Even then, however, he was beginning to think in terms of last resorts:

... *I am willing to pledge myself* [italics his] that if the time should ever come that the voluntary agencies of the country together with the local and state governments are unable to find resources with which to prevent hunger and suffering in my country, *I will ask the aid of every resource of the Federal government because I would no more see starvation amongst our countrymen than would any Senator or Congressman....*

Would we have to have a Russian famine to convince the President?

Backers of direct federal aid could take little immediate comfort from Hoover's apparent concession. But shortly after, with the blessing of the President and the reluctant acquiescence of Senate progressives, Congress passed a measure that could be interpreted as food relief, appropriating $20,000,000 for "agricultural rehabilitation" loans. Though not a mention of food appeared in the bill, the Secretary of Agriculture, a former Missouri Ford dealer named Arthur M. Hyde, admitted in a guarded telephone interview with a reporter that farmers could spend the money any way they pleased. But borrowers had to provide good security for the loans, which meant in effect that only those who had not been bankrupted by the drought were eligible. That the money benefited those who least needed it seemed beside the point: the administration had won the battle of principle. As the House majority leader, John Q. Tilson of Connecticut, said, "It's not a dole. Remember, it's not a dole."

On the face of things Hoover could justify his stand: by March, 1931, the Red Cross announced that it had fed or clothed 2,000,000 persons in twenty-one states. But that figure was somewhat less impressive when broken down into individual cases. A man could live, but just barely, on a Red Cross handout of forty to fifty cents' worth of food per week, with some cans of tomato and salmon—supposed to strengthen gastric tubes—thrown in if he was suffering from pellagra. Clearly private relief, even on this heroic scale, made only a dent in the problem. In Mississippi the Red Cross fed 150,000 drought victims that winter; nobody knew how many thousands more were slowly starving. The first Red Cross aid did not arrive until January; by then the need was so great that relief seekers walked barefoot for miles in the cold weather. A family of six in Bolivar County got $11.67 in groceries per month, or less than $2.00 a person, while a mule could receive $8.00 in feed for the same period through government loans, which was an example of life imitating a wisecrack. The state government had done nothing all this time: the governor, Theodore G. Bilbo, would not call a special session of the legislature because members refused to sign promises not to impeach him.

Arkansas remained the worst sufferer: as of the middle of February, the Red Cross was feeding 519,000 persons. The *Times* reported late in January that roads around the town of Marked Tree were "clogged with wagons and buggies, not automobiles, and men and women walking with sacks of flour on their shoulders and pails of lard in their hands...." But Red Cross aid must never have reached the three members of one family in Hot Springs, who apparently died of malnutrition at about that same time. (The precise reasons for such deaths, recorded under a variety of related causes, from heart failure to pellagra, are impossible to trace.) Small jokes told a great deal: rabbits—scarce, too, that winter—were known as Hoover hogs, and there was the recipe for a turnip sandwich: "three slices of turnip and put one in the middle." The humor was no thinner than the reality. Russell Owen of the *Times* noted the following exchange between a Red Cross worker and an old farmer in the relief station at Wynne, Arkansas. The farmer, a pale man with eyes a little inflamed, needed food, but it had been a struggle for him to apply for charity.

"I didn't want to come around, but I heard the others were getting something, and we are pretty low at home," he said.

"Time to pocket your pride?"

"Yes, that's it."

The Red Cross worker asked how much food he had left at home. A little flour, some meal, and a few potatoes, the farmer told him.

And meat?

"I haven't had any meat in a year." He seemed astonished, Owen said, to be asked such a foolish question.

A chairman of a local branch of an Arkansas unemployment bureau claimed that in his county alone 23,000 out of a total of 26,000 had to be fed: "From last March until this March," he said, "we in these parts had but little over one inch rainfall, so made our fourth failure...." His job was mainly to take over from the Red Cross in situations that it was not prepared to handle. For example, what was most needed in the spring of 1931 was seed corn, and he managed to obtain a freight car of

The miniature-golf craze was so widespread that in 1930 everyone understood this agricultural obstacle course and the weary farmer who had "played this game for years."

surplus corn donated by friends in Iowa. (Why, people wondered, wasn't the federal government this resourceful?) He paid for the carrying charges, $250, out of his own pocket; the Red Cross would only pay for corn used as feed for animals. He was also helping to provide free lunches for schoolchildren, both white and black. He wrote:

... The Red Cross has been allowing only three and one-half cents a day per individual, and that is being cut down now. Many of the county children were making their noonday luncheon out of hickory nuts picked up in the woods. We are now, through Red Cross and private donations, feeding over 75 percent of the children in the county one hot meal a day. This is the only meal many of these children get. There are so many ways we can use funds to help the destitute that do not come under the rigid Red Cross rules....

Applicants were too often snooped on and lectured to, and had to submit to what amounted to a means test—a soul-destroying advance on the British, who did not initiate their version of such personal prying until the fall. In Kentucky, Edmund Wilson found that if a man owned two cows, no matter how dry they were or how hungry he was, he would probably be denied relief, on the theory that he could sell one. Wilson overheard the plea of a good-hearted lady relief worker to a hill farmer in such a fix: "Well, I'll give you an order, but I don't want you to tell anybody about it—please don't mention it to anybody."

In the end, rain did as much good as the Red Cross or the government, though its help, too, was insufficient. There were some heavy downpours all through the Ohio and Mississippi valleys in March and again in April. As a media fad at least, the great drought was over. In some parts of the country it was actually worse in 1931 than it had been the previous year, though it received scant notice since fewer people were involved. The Great Plains were entering one of their periodic dry spells, and it was no coincidence that by the winter of 1931–32 the sky would be blackened by the first dust storms.

Time and more than a few cloudbursts were needed for the groundwater supplies that fed wells and springs and grass roots to build up again. As the geographer and conservationist J. Russell Smith warned in the spring of 1931, prospects for the farmer were not bright: "His hay field is without grass. His wheat is in bad order. His haymows are emptier than ever before at this time of year, his flocks and herds are reduced. His mortgages are bigger; his notes at the bank are more pressing; his credit is lower, to say nothing of low prices caused by the slump." Smith's gloomy forecast was borne out. To cite one statistic of this total environmental collapse: gross farm income, which had been $9.4 billion in the drought year of 1930, would fall to $6.9 billion in 1931, a loss of two and a half billion dollars. To put that another way, the average American farmer would net just $342 for a whole year's work.

Arkansas had a fortunate summer on the whole; its disasters for once were only the normal personal ones of the Depression. Crops were better than usual, and in a special Thanksgiving message in November the President could speak of courage and energy surmounting hardship, and of the blessings of Almighty Providence. He compared this day to the first Thanksgiving, when the Plymouth Colony had celebrated a harvest after months of near-famine. That was the closest he ever came to admitting that the drought had really caused near-famine. England, Arkansas, was mostly forgotten by that time; surprisingly there had been no immediate rush to follow H. C. Coney's example. Maybe people were too demoralized; maybe their sense of isolation was too acute for collective action. That sense of isolation had struck Russell Owen with haunting impact: "Not an isolation

This cartoonist seems to feel compassion for the hard-working though ineffectual President, surrounded as he was by a chorus of abuse for the sickness of the economy.

LEFT: BILLY IRELAND IN THE COLUMBUS, (OHIO) *Dispatch*; RIGHT: JERRY COSTELLO IN THE *Knickerbocker News*, ALBANY, N.Y.

of distance or of time or inaccessibility, but one which is expressed in a breakdown of commerce and trade. When a man on a mortgaged and barren farm has no money he cannot order anything; when his food gives out, he cannot get more. . . . He is lost in a world of plenty. Civilization has failed him except as it gives him charity."

But the England incident did find its way into the Depression mythology, largely via a story that young Whittaker Chambers published in the March, 1931, issue of the Communist *New Masses*. The story was called, in the prescribed clarion manner of proletarian fiction, "You Can Make Out Their Voices," and soon became one of the radical classics of the 1930's. His was the Arkansas of a revolutionary dreamworld. The voice of the bourgeois villain issues "from the small slit of his lips," and his daughter has "big breasts, glasses and a gold incisor." (For some reason the other bad lady in the story, a Red Cross worker, also wears glasses: she is the one who exclaims, "We ought to spread some bags of flour on the counter. There's nothing like it for psychological effect.") The farmer-hero turns out to be a home-grown agrarian Communist, who directs the looting of Red Cross headquarters and then leads his band of embattled farmers into the hills to await the inevitable coming of the capitalist militia. But first he sends away his two sons—"East, to the comrades."

Lincoln Steffens told Chambers that his story was a model of proletarian art, the eminent Soviet authority on American literature A. Elistratova praised it, and Hallie Flannagan, director of the Vassar College experimental theatre, produced it as a play there. But the final judgment belongs to the party critic who wrote that "Can You Hear Their Voices?"—the name had been changed along the way—"eclipses anything that can be written about it."

The real H. C. Coney would have been miscast in the leading role. Early in the spring of 1931 a reporter found him living in his shack on the outskirts of England. Little had changed for him. The house needed a paint job, and the roof leaked; inside, old newspapers were pasted on the walls to keep out the wind. On the mantelpiece the reporter saw an atlas, a Bible, and a cheap print of the Last Supper, partly covered by an old cylinder gasket. Coney told him that the farmers had grown "more sociable-like" since the invasion of England: "I think that three winters like this one would see them organized." But he was mainly concerned with getting a government loan. The regional office at Memphis, Tennessee, had approved his request for $195 to tide him over until his cotton crop matured, but he had to wait for final certification as to his general character by a county committee. The local authorities cancelled the advance. *They* had not forgotten him. ☆

Robert Cowley, the managing editor of our sister publication, HORIZON, *is at work on a book about the period between the First and Second World Wars. The book from which this article is adapted is to be called* False Armistice, *and will be published by Simon and Schuster.*

HOOVER'S SURPRISING NEW FRIENDS

Historical reputations have strange, chameleonlike lives, changing hues with changing times. Herbert Hoover has long occupied a prominent role in the demonology of American liberalism. It would seem natural, therefore, that the historians of the New Left, who are unsparingly critical of most of the nation's past leaders, would be even harsher in their judgment of the Great Engineer. Yet astonishingly enough, Hoover's views have won respect from some "revisionist" historians, as the remarks below reveal. Professor William Appleman Williams, of Oregon State University, one of the earliest New Left scholars, was asked by AMERICAN HERITAGE *for a comment on the foregoing article and replied with the following estimate of Hoover—which leads to intriguing speculations on what other once-condemned American conservatives may become tomorrow's revisionist heroes.*

The inside truth is that H. C. Hoover is also H. C. Coney. Both were men caught up in doing what they had to do, and both had a handle on part of the truth. Coney was right. Children and women and men need to be helped when the system (*any* system) fails to reward their commitment and their labor. Indeed, they must be helped: he was beautiful in the way he cut through to his truth and did what he had to do.

But Hoover was also right. He recognized a crucial point before it was demonstrated. That was his beauty, though we have never fully understood it—or honored him. Hoover told us that if we (the neighbors of the stricken) cannot be roused to provide such help, and if the way the government helps them in lieu of our direct assistance is not handled *very* carefully, then make no mistake and play no games: there will be hell to pay for the help they get.

Hoover perceived the outlines of that inferno. He feared there would be bureaucratic statism that would devalue the human beings it claimed to save; that there would be imperialism in the name of welfare; and that there would be violence in the name of peace. We now know those were legitimate fears.

That does not change the need for direct relief. But it does help us understand more fully why H. C. Coney could tighten the screws on H. C. Hoover. And it does give us more to turn over in our minds as we reflect on the episode.

The point is to get both truths together. Meaning that unless you and I decide that she and he are at least as important as us, then we all are going down the memory hole together. The time is long past for passing the buck to the government.
—*William Appleman Williams*

The Spies Who Went out in the Cold
CONTINUED FROM PAGE 55

Jones and a relative of the Weston innkeeper, "seemed a little sour" when they entered. And well he might have been. On January 27 the Worcester County Convention had "earnestly recommended" that the inhabitants of the county "shun his house and person, and treat him with the contempt he deserves." Jones soon became friendly, but neither he nor the soldiers directly disclosed their sympathies. When asked what he could offer for breakfast, Jones answered "tea or anything else we chose—that was an open confession what he was; but for fear he might be imprudent, we did not tell him who we were, tho' we were certain he knew it."

The next day presented a new obstacle: the Sunday blue laws. New Englanders either went to all-day church services or stayed indoors. Anyone who dared step out was questioned by the town watch, "so that thinking we could not stand the examination so well, we thought it prudent to stay at home, where we wrote and corrected our sketches." In the late afternoon, after services were finally over, Browne and De Birniere ventured out around the town and the hills surrounding it, "sketched every thing we desired, and returned to the town without being seen." De Birniere, in fact, drew up plans for a fortress and encampment on one of the hills commanding Worcester.

At about eight o'clock that night Jones came to the soldiers' room to say two gentlemen wanted to speak to them. Who were they? Jones replied that they "wou'd be safe in their company." Still clinging to his cover, De Birniere said they didn't doubt it, as they hoped that gentlemen "who travelled merely to see the country and stretch our limbs" would be treated civilly as long as they behaved themselves. An hour later Jones returned to say the two visitors had gone away, "but had begged him to let us know, as they knew us to be officers of the army," that all the Loyalists in the town of Petersham had been "disarmed by the rebels, and that they threatened to do the same at Worcester in a very little time." Even after the landlord shared a bottle and talked politics with them, the soldiers did not drop their guard. When he "told us that none but a few friends to government knew we were in town," the officers replied that they did not care "whether they did or not, tho' we thought very differently." Obviously, Browne and De Birniere were frightened; if they had not been, they would certainly have seized the opportunity to pick up information from Worcester residents. They decided to get out of town at daybreak.

The spies had entered Worcester on Saturday by way of Grafton; they left on Monday by the Shrewsbury road. They passed through Shrewsbury without being seen, but were then "overtaken by a horseman who examined us very attentively, and especially [De Birniere], whom he looked at from head to foot as if he wanted to know [him] again." Then the horseman "rode off pretty hard and took the Marlborough road." Alarmed by this, the soldiers switched back to their previous road to Framingham, rationalizing that it would probably be the one the army would use anyway. It was lucky they did, for the horseman was Timothy Bigelow, a Worcester blacksmith who was a captain of the minutemen and a member of the Provincial Congress. Bigelow warned the Marlborough patriots to be on the lookout for three men who walked like soldiers.

When the three spies arrived back at Buckminster's tavern in Framingham, about six o'clock, they found a company of militia drilling outside. "We did not feel very easy at seeing such a number so very near us," De Birniere admitted, "however, they did not know who we were, and took little or no notice of us." After they completed their drill, the commander, to De Birniere's great amusement, addressed his troops. He advised them to exercise patience, coolness, and bravery (which, De Birniere noted, they were much in need of) and "particularly told them they would always conquer if they did not break, and recommended them to charge us cooly, and wait for our fire, and every thing would succeed with them—quotes Caesar and Pompey, brigadiers Putnam and Ward,* and all such great men; put them in mind of Cape Breton, and all the battles they had gained for His Majesty in the last war, and observed that the regulars must have been ruined but for them.—After so learned and spirited an harangue, he dismissed the parade, and the whole company came into the house and drank until nine o'clock, and then returned to their respective homes full of pot-valour."

De Birniere might have been less amused if he had reflected that the New Englanders had captured the French citadels at Port Royal and Louisbourg in three different wars or that the advice given by their commander was perfectly sound. Furthermore, although De Birniere took several opportunities to show his regular's scorn for American militia, if he found anything funny about the Framingham company's drill, he did not write it down. Seven weeks later every man of Framingham's three companies was on hand to harass the redcoats, De Birniere and Browne among them, as they fled from Concord back to Boston.

No one disturbed the spies in Framingham, nor as they walked back to Weston on Tuesday, February 28, "having fine weather and a beautiful country to travel through." Their spirits were so heightened that when they got to the Golden Ball tavern and their friend Mr. Jones, they ignored "several hints from the family not to go any more into the country." Perhaps they felt sheepish because a passing horseman had frightened them off the Marlborough road. Perhaps "pot-valour" worked on British

*Israel Putnam and Artemas Ward were veterans of the French and Indian War who commanded the armies of Connecticut and Massachusetts, respectively. Ward commanded the American Army until George Washington took over in July, 1775.

officers as well as on American militiamen. They decided that, after all, they should examine the main Boston-Worcester road through Sudbury and Marlborough, to the point where they had left it ten miles outside of Worcester.

The next morning was "very cloudy and threatened bad weather." March 1 would get a great deal darker and more threatening for Browne and De Birniere before it was over. They put their papers in order and sent John off with them to Boston, "so that if they did stop and search us, they would not get our papers." This was a wise precaution, of course, but it deprived the officers of John's common sense and ability to talk to the local people.

At noon it began to snow, but Browne and De Birniere had an early lunch anyway, "in hopes the weather would clear up." Had they been Yankees, the spies would have recognized the signs of that spectacular phenomenon of New England meteorology, the northeaster. At two o'clock the snow let up a little, so they decided to set out for Marlborough, about sixteen miles away. "We found the roads very bad, every step up to our ankles," but that at least kept other travellers inside. They passed through Sudbury and over a "causeway . . . across a great swamp," and, as it was snowing hard again, escaped notice until a horseman overtook them three miles outside Marlborough. Where were they coming from, he wanted to know.

Weston. Did they live there? No. Where did they live? "As we found there was no evading his questions, we told him we lived at Boston; he then asked us where we were going, we told him to Marlborough, to see a friend, (as we intended to go to Mr. Barnes's, a gentleman to whom we were recommended, and a friend to government;) he then asked if we were in the army, we said not, but were a good deal alarmed at his asking us that question." After a few more "rather impertinent questions," the horseman rode off toward Marlborough to spread word of their arrival.

When they entered the town, "the people came out of their houses (tho' it snowed and blew very hard) to look at us." A baker asked Captain Browne: "Where are you going master?" Browne replied, "to see Mr. Barnes." That, if nothing else, would have tipped off their sympathies. Henry Barnes, a prosperous applejack distiller and merchant, was a notorious Tory who had been on the outs with the local patriots ever since he broke the nonimportation agreement in 1770.

At Barnes's, Browne and De Birniere started to apologize for arriving unannounced and "discovering to him that we were officers in disguise." Barnes stopped their explanation. Not only he, but everybody else in town, knew who they were. In fact, on Monday night, a hot welcome had been prepared for them by "a party of liberty people" who had been warned by Captain Bigelow, the horseman who had looked De Birniere over so carefully. Was there a safe tavern where they could stay? No, Barnes answered, the town was very violent and his was the only house where they were not sure to meet trouble. Had they spoken to anyone when they entered town? They told Barnes about Browne's encounter with the baker. That was bad. The baker was an ardent patriot and had a deserter living

101

in his house. Browne asked the deserter's name. It was Swain, a drummer. That tore it. Browne "knew him too well"; less than a month ago Swain had been Browne's own company drummer! "We asked Mr. Barnes if they did get us into their hands, what they would do with us; he did not seem to like to answer; we asked him again, he then said we knew the people very well, that we might expect the worst of treatment from them." Barnes did not have to elaborate; every Tory and redcoat knew about the "modern punishment," tar and feathers.

At this point Barnes was called to the door. His caller was Dr. Samuel Curtis, a member of the local Committee of Correspondence. Curtis casually said he had dropped by for a bite of supper, though he had not been in Barnes's house for two years, and a high Son of Liberty was unlikely to be making a social call on the town's leading Tory. Barnes said he was sorry, but he had company. Then Dr. Curtis asked one of Barnes's children who her father's visitors were. "The child innocently answered that she had asked her pappa, but he told her it was not her business." That was all Curtis needed. He hurried off to tell his fellow committeemen.

Browne and De Birniere decided that Marlborough was too hot for them. They would rest for two or three hours, then sneak out of town at midnight. But just as they were sitting down to supper, Barnes rushed in to tell them that his servants reported a delegation of townspeople on its way. No time even to eat. Snatching up a bit of bread, the spies rushed out the back door past the stables and fled down a back lane that would take them again to the Sudbury road a quarter mile out of town. They had been in Barnes's house for twenty minutes.

They had left just in time. A few weeks later, when Barnes himself was forced to flee to Boston, he reported that Dr. Curtis had returned with the rest of the Committee of Correspondence and demanded to see the British officers. Barnes said they were not officers, but some of his wife's relatives from Penobscot, headed for Lancaster, and besides, they had already left. The committeemen "searched his house from top to bottom, looked under the beds and in their cellars, and when they found we were gone, they told him if they had caught us in his house, they would have pulled it about his ears."

In the meantime Browne and De Birniere were making the best speed they could while "it snowed and blew as much as ever I see it in my life." They got as far as the causeway at Sudbury, where they went off into the woods to "eat a bit of bread that we took from Mr. Barnes's and eat a little snow to wash it down." This is undoubtedly how they missed being spotted by one of the horsemen sent out on every road when it was discovered that the officers had left Barnes's. Back on the road they walked but a hundred yards when a man came out of a house and said to Browne: "What do you think will become of you now?" They were sure they were caught, especially as they still had to cross the causeway. Then they were certain they would be stopped in Sudbury village. They

102

"met three or four horsemen, from whom we expected a few shot," but as they drew near, the riders "opened to the right and left and . . . let us pass through without taking any notice." Either they were concealed by the blowing snow or, more likely, those particular horsemen were not among the ones looking for the two British officers.

At last they got back to the Golden Ball in Weston, "very much fatigued, after walking thirty-two miles between two o'clock and half after ten at night, through a road that every step we sunk up to the ankles, and it blowing and drifting snow all the way." Mr. Jones was glad to see them. He was sure they would run into trouble, he told the soldiers, "as they had been watching for us sometime," but had not thought it proper to give more than hints as warnings. The weary travellers "went to bed and slept as sound as men could do," when they have walked thirty-two miles through a snowstorm and finished off a bottle of mulled Madeira wine.

The next morning, Thursday, March 2, Browne and De Birniere set off for Boston. This time they crossed the Charles, so that they could avoid going through Watertown again, and arrived at the fortifications on Boston Neck at noon. General Gage and his aides were at Boston Neck, but they did not recognize Browne and De Birniere, nor did several of their friends when they finally got into town. Eight days on the road in the hypervaried weather of late winter in New England had, at least, perfected their disguise.

General Gage must have found their sketches and reports satisfactory, for on March 20 Browne, De Birniere, and probably John as well were ordered on a similar mission to Concord. They got to Concord, by way of Roxbury, Brookline, and Weston, "without any kind of insult being offered to us." They were not, however, unobserved. They asked a woman to direct them to the home of Daniel Bliss, one of the town's leading Tories. Shortly after they arrived at Bliss's, the woman "came in crying, and told us they swore if she did not leave town, they would tar and feather her for directing Tories in their road." Bliss, himself, had just the opposite problem: "they had sent him word they would not let him go out of town alive that morning." Bliss had collected a great deal of accurate information about where cannon and provisions were stored in Concord. The soldiers assured him that "if he would come with us we would take care of him, as we were three and all well armed."

Bliss gratefully accepted and showed the soldiers another road, through Lexington. De Birniere noted that the road out of Concord was "very open and good for six miles, the next five a little enclosed (there is one very bad place in these five miles)." They passed through Lexington, then Menotomy (Arlington), and Cambridge, and so on to Boston without trouble.

The next time Ensign De Birniere travelled that route was on April 19, 1775. He was guiding a column of redcoats, commanded by Lieutenant Colonel Francis Smith, that had as its objective the stores in Concord that Browne and De Birniere had learned about a month earlier. De Birniere saw Captain John Parker's minutemen lined up on Lexington Green, saw them fall under a hail of fire from British muskets. He helped destroy some stores at Barrett's farm beyond the North Bridge in Concord, although "we did not find so much as we expected," and returned to the bridge to find that the American Revolution was now a shooting war. De Birniere saw his troops begin "to run rather than retreat in order" when they came to the "one very bad place" outside of Lexington he had noted in March. Here the remnants of Captain Parker's company repaid the redcoats with interest, as they poured a withering fire from Pine Hill.

De Birniere survived the rout of Gage's only real attempt to break out of Boston and the slaughter at Bunker Hill in June. When the British left Boston forever, on March 17, 1776, among the things they left behind were De Birniere's maps, his plan for a military post in Worcester, and his account of his days as a spy. The last was "printed for the information and amusement of the curious" by J. Gill of Court Street, Boston, in 1779. Nearly two hundred years later it should remind us that the American Revolution was not something that started on April 19, 1775—that was merely the shooting phase. The "hearts and minds of the people," as John Adams was fond of saying, were already made up.

Neil R. Stout is associate professor of history at the University of Vermont. He recently completed a book, The Royal Navy in America 1760–1775, *for the U.S. Naval Institute and is currently working on another that focusses on the year before the Revolution broke out—1774.*

Quebec
CONTINUED FROM PAGE 15

main body of Montgomery's troops was approaching, and he had ordered his troops to evacuate Montreal. He had eleven ships of varying sizes, and their captains prepared for the run down the river that was certain to be strongly challenged. At dusk the vessels—loaded with ammunition, supplies, and more than a hundred fighting men, including nonprofessionals—weighed anchor and moved down the St. Lawrence under fire from Rebel guns on the south shore.

The next day one of the ships ran aground, and the little fleet had to heave to until it could be cleared. Then, that night, the easterly gale that had held Arnold down opposite Quebec roared up the river past Sorel. The British vessels had no alternative but to drop anchor and ride out the storm. But Carleton's luck was bad. On the sixteenth, five days after they had left Montreal, the wind was still in the east. Until it veered west, the vessels would have no hope of running the gauntlet through the long narrows at Sorel—with Rebel guns pounding them at close range from both sides.

At last Carleton decided that he should go on ahead of the rest of his force and try to escape past the Rebels so that he could assume command in Quebec. Dressed as a Canadian peasant habitant, the Governor was transported by a whaler with muffled oars through the nine-mile narrows of the Berthier Islands. As the craft moved into the flickering pools of illumination from the Rebel fires on the banks, the crew stopped rowing and crouched down so that the boat resembled one of the big hunks of rotten timber that were always floating downstream.

Just past the town of Three Rivers the fugitives found at anchor a British armed brig, which took them the rest of the way to Quebec. By then, the British flotilla of vessels, held immobile by the wind, had been captured by the Rebels. More than a hundred fighting men—many of them British regulars needed in Quebec—had been taken prisoner.

As soon as Carleton assumed command of the city, he took action against the Rebel sympathizers, who were a constant threat. By proclamation he ordered every male resident to enroll in the militia, quit the city, or risk prosecution as a spy. By the end of November his garrison of sailors and civilians—supported by his few precious regulars—amounted to eighteen hundred untrained, undrilled men. The numbers that Montgomery could deploy have been the subject of conflict. There were probably about a thousand Americans—Arnold's men plus the three hundred Montgomery brought with him from Montreal. Some historians have doubted the presence of Canadians, but according to reports in Quebec at the time, they added at least some hundreds to the Rebel General's force.

Tensely, during those last days of November, the garrison in Quebec waited for the return of the Rebels. Snow fell heavily. Ice swirled down the river. Rumors abounded.

On December 2 a man was reported for making alarmist speeches to the superstitious and highly credulous habitants. Already they had been astonished by the light clothing worn by Arnold's men after the journey that, with some grounds, they regarded as miraculous. The *provocateur* had played on the French word *toile* ("linen") and suggested it should be *tôle* ("iron plate"). The belief that the Americans were clad in vests of musket-proof sheet iron was soon spreading fast.

On Carleton's orders one of Quebec's huge gates was hauled open. Drummers lined the entrance on both sides. A jeering crowd gathered to watch. To the noise of the rolling drums, with the beat emphasizing every step he took, the man was made to walk out of the town.

On December 4 reports filtered through the city that Montgomery had joined Arnold at Pointe aux Trembles with "many cannon" and "4,500 men." As usual, the rumor turned out to be an exaggeration, but on the following day the sentries on the wall saw in the distance the long American column—the combined forces of Montgomery and Arnold—approaching across the snow on the Plains of Abraham. Not long afterward the bateaux carrying the guns and ammunition were spotted on the river by a naval patrol boat.

The two American forces deployed before the town. Arnold's men—who had now abandoned their awesome "*tôle*" shirts for captured British winter clothing that Montgomery had brought up—occupied the suburbs of St. Roche to the north. Montgomery's troops camped on the plain to the west. For two days little happened.

On December 7 Montgomery made an attempt to demand surrender. He had copies of a letter to Carleton attached to arrows and fired into the town—with some apparent success, for Carleton sent one home to London. "I am well acquainted with your situation . . . ," it warned, taunting that the walls were "incapable of defense, manned with a motley crew of sailors the greatest part our friends, of citizens who wish to see us within the walls. . . . The impossibility of relief and the certain prospect of wanting every necessary of life, should your opponents confine their missions to a simple blockade, point out that absurdity of resistance. . . ."

Carleton had much the same view of his hopes of saving the city, but he himself had besieged Quebec and he had learned from Montcalm's error. There was to be no sallying forth to battle on the Plains. He knew that the classic assault tactic—approaching the walls in trenches—was impractical in the frozen ground. Even with his amateur garrison he could insure that Quebec would be a hard place to storm.

By the morning of the sixteenth, after the city had been under heavy shelling for six days, the guards on the walls near the Palace Gate sounded the alarm. Carleton, sleeping in his clothes, was awakened with the news that six hundred men were approaching from St. Roche. The drummers pounded out the beat to arms. The cathedral bells pealed urgently. Throughout the town the garrison hurried to their posts—and peered through a heavy snowstorm into the blackness beyond the light cast by the lanterns jutting from the ramparts. But the attack never came.

Four days later Thomas Ainsley, a collector of customs serving as a militia captain, wrote in his journal: "Montgomery is reported to have said that he would dine in Quebec or in Hell at Christmas. We are determined that he shall not dine in town and be his own master.... The weather is very severe indeed. No man, after having been exposed to to the air about 10 minutes, could handle his arms to do execution. One's senses are benumbed. Whenever they attack us, it will be in mild weather.... Ice and snow, now heaped up in places [against the walls] where we have reckoned the weakest, are exceeding strong."

Two days later it was still bitterly cold. Late that night Joshua Wolfe—a clerk who had been taken prisoner by the Rebels—escaped by getting his jailer drunk. He reported that the Rebels planned to storm the town the following night—the twenty-third. Montgomery, he said, was having trouble persuading his men "to undertake a step so desperate." He had promised them £200 each in plunder. They had five hundred scaling ladders made "in a very clumsy manner."

"Can these men pretend that there is a possibility of approaching our walls laden with ladders, sinking to the middle every step in the snow?" mused Ainsley. Carleton was not so skeptical. That night a thousand men were posted on the walls, waiting, staring across the snow, until the sun rose.

It was a wise precaution, for on the following day a Rebel deserter ran up to the St. John's Gate on the west of the Upper Town, fired his musket into the air, clubbed it to indicate surrender, and asked for admission. Because the guards had orders not to open the gates, they hauled him onto the wall by ropes. He reported that the attack had indeed been planned, but Montgomery had postponed it when he realized that Wolfe's escape would raise the alarm. They would surely attack that night, the deserter warned, unless his own escape deterred them.

But nothing happened—although the guards "saw many lights all around us which we took for signals." The weather, meantime, turned milder—which, so Ainsley conjectured, would make attack more likely. However, as it later appeared, Montgomery planned to attack under cover of bad weather.

On New Year's Eve the weather changed. By the evening it was snowing heavily and an icy wind was chilling the sentries on duty.

At 4 A.M. the officer of the guard, Captain Malcolm Fraser of the Emigrants, trudged along the wall, with his body bent before the gale, on his routine rounds. As he approached the posts at the southern end of the walls, he saw what looked like musket flashes on the heights, but he was puzzled because he could not hear any shots. He questioned the sentries facing Cape Diamond, which overlooked the St. Lawrence, and they said they had seen the flashes for some time. He moved back along the wall and asked the guards at the next post about the lights. "Like lamps in the street" was how one man described them. Fraser guessed that they were lanterns and that the Rebels were forming for attack. He ordered the alarm.

Again the drummers pounded out the call to arms. Once more the bells of the city clanged out an insistent warning through the noise of the storm. Officers ran through the streets bawling to the militia to turn out. Men tumbled from beds on which they were lying in their clothes, grabbed their guns, and hurried to their posts. Two rockets whooshed skyward in quick succession from Cape Diamond. Then the firing started. Rebels, shooting from the cover of rocks on high ground by Cape Diamond, were only eighty yards from the posts on the ramparts and at a level that was almost as high.

However, by firing, the Rebels inevitably exposed their positions. "The flashes from their muskets made their heads visible," recorded Ainsley, "[and] we briskly returned the fire."

Farther north, on the wall by St. John's Gate, the gunners had fired flaming shot to illuminate the approaches beyond the circles of light thrown by the lanterns thrust out from the ramparts on long poles. Anxiously, they stared through the snowstorm toward the suburb of St. John, which was a good starting point for an assault.

The attack came fast—men running from the far blackness of the houses toward the gate, the flickering fireballs striking from them dark, giant moving shadows.

The big guns crashed out, the muzzles flaring white flame, and jerked back on their carriages until they strained the retaining ropes. Between the cannons the militiamen lined the walls, shooting volley after volley at their attackers.

Still the Rebels came on until they were almost at the big gates. Then, suddenly, they broke and ran. It was, so the British discovered later, only a diversion, with no intention to follow through; but to the men on the walls it had looked determined enough.

Meanwhile, the men posted above the Palace Gate, on the north of the city facing the St. Roche suburb, were suddenly alerted. Here the walls merged into tall buildings, the backs of which overlooked the St. Charles River way below. At the foot of the buildings, above the wave-washed rocks, was a path that led down around the eastern edge of the town to the port.

Shells from the Rebel mortars in St. Roche had been falling for some time. Now, suddenly, the guards over the gate—their attention diverted until then by the noise of attack on the west—noticed in the dim light a long column of men in single file passing silently from the direction of St. Roche down the rock path to the harbor. The column, already going by below them, was too close for cannon fire. But the militiamen opened up with their muskets.

Seamen from the ships in the port were manning the eastern windows of the Hôtel de Dieu immediately above the path. As the Rebel file passed below them—so Ainsley reported—"they were exposed to a dreadful fire of small arms which the sailors poured down on them."

The pathway was rough, heaped with rugged piles of ice and soft snow. Fireballs, lobbed from the town, illuminated the long line of slipping, sliding men, some of them carrying scaling ladders, as they worked their way down toward the harbor. To the defenders above, they made easy targets. Gaps were ripped in the file by the musket shot; men jerked and toppled into the snow.

But still, despite the heavy shooting from above them, the Rebel column went on, stepping over their dead and wounded, toward the Lower Town.

The Lower Town, the underbelly of the fortress city, was—as Carleton fully realized—where Quebec's weakness truly lay. Log palisades and barriers—supported by guns and men with muskets—blocked the streets that led from the wharves and from paths such as the one to the east that Arnold's men were now descending under heavy fire.

There was another route that stretched out of the Lower Town on the other side—this one to the west, along the rock face of the towering Cape Diamond to Wolfe's Cove. Narrow, cluttered with snow and ice, bordered on one side by bare cliff, it dropped sheerly to the St. Lawrence below.

The main defense of this entrance to the Lower Town was in a blockhouse formed out of an old brewery building that commanded the upward curving roadway from behind a log barrier. Here a small battery of three-pounder guns had been set up with their barrels jutting out of the windows. To man and support this battery with muskets were some fifty men. Most of them were Quebec residents, but they were backed up by eight seamen from the ships in the port and a Royal Artillery sergeant, the only professional among them. In command of the post was one Captain Barnsfair, master of a merchantman.

From the windows of the blockhouse Barnsfair and his men stared out toward the bend in the road, only faintly visible in the early dawn light and falling snow. The gunners had lighted matches waiting ready.

Then they saw them. At first it was just a suspicion, a sense that there was movement out there in the gray storm, followed by the certainty—a group of shadowy figures with the snow swirling round them. They appeared to be an advance unit, for they stopped as soon as they had seen the blockhouse, as though waiting for the main body to catch up.

Tensely, the men in the blockhouse watched the attackers. "We shall not fire," Barnsfair warned, "until we can be sure of doing execution."

At last the Rebels began to advance slowly. The gunners in the blockhouse waited for Barnsfair's order. As they walked, the Americans scuffed the snow with their feet, looking almost unreal in the half-light. When they were about fifty yards away, they stopped again, "as though in consultation." Then, one of them moved forward, peered at the barricade and the blockhouse for a moment, and returned to the others.

Again, for a few minutes the Rebels seemed to be discussing what to do. Suddenly, as a group, they made a dash, all of them running fast to storm the barricade. Still Barnsfair waited, watching the Rebels advancing swiftly. Then, at last, as the nearest men were almost at the barricade, he gave the order: "Fire!"

The gunners put their matches to the touchholes, and the explosions as the guns went off in those close confines were deafening. The musketeers squeezed their triggers and swiftly reloaded. "Our musketry and guns," Ainsley wrote, "continued to sweep the avenue leading to the battery for some minutes. When the smoke cleared, there was not a soul to be seen."

Not on their feet—but thirteen bodies lay in the snow, and two of them were groaning. The slaughter of the close-range firing seemed to convince the Rebels that the post was held too strongly, for they did not attack again.

Carleton was directing the defense of the city from the Upper Town in the Place d'Armes, the parade ground, where the mobile reserve was held waiting. Already he had ordered an artillery officer to hurry down with a militia company to support Barnsfair, who had been reported under heavy attack. Now, he received news of the assault from the east side of the

Lower Town that was far more serious. Some schoolboys hurried into the Place d'Armes, shouting: "The enemy's in possession of the Sault-au-Matelot."

The Sault-au-Matelot was a very narrow street that led from the waterside into the Lower Town. It was the route for any attack round the outside of the city from the direction of the St. Charles. For this reason it was strongly defended—with a high log barricade, well manned and armed with two cannons—at the point where the Rebels would enter it.

It should have been able to withstand a sustained attack, at least until a message could be gotten to Carleton asking for support. The information that the enemy had broken through so quickly was, therefore, very surprising. (Later, it was charged that the officer in command of the post was a rebel spy.) But the critical aspect of the news was that, since the Sault-au-Matelot led directly into the main part of the Lower Town, once the Rebels gained control of that street, they would have a very strong base from which to assault the Upper Town. Arnold understood this, and had decided to make the Sault-au-Matelot the focal point of his main attack.

Carleton was an experienced fighter. Swiftly, when the facts were confirmed, he planned his strategy. The Sault-au-Matelot had cannon-supported barricades at each end. Although the Rebels had broken through the first barricade, they had evidently paused in the street before the second. It was vital to Carleton's defense planning that they should be held at this point.

Carleton dispatched Colonel Caldwell of the Quebec militia to reinforce the defense at the vital barricade at the end of the Sault-au-Matelot. With him the colonel took Carleton's handful of fusiliers and a force of militia and sailors.

At the same time the Governor ordered another strong detachment to march out of the city through the Palace Gate in the north wall of the town and down the same rock path above the St. Charles that the Rebels had traversed earlier under fire from the sailors in the Hôtel de Dieu, and to attack from the rear.

The plan to trap the Rebels in the narrow Sault-au-Matelot was brilliant, but it depended completely on Caldwell's holding the barricade. He arrived barely in time. The Rebels were just about to assault the stockade that blocked the twenty-foot-wide street. Already, scaling ladders were propped against the barrier.

Caldwell had more room in which to deploy his forces than had the Rebels. The road curved upward away from the Sault-au-Matelot and then split into two branches. Swiftly, he ordered the fusiliers into line, backs against the houses and facing the barricade with fixed bayonets. From there they could fire at the Rebels as they mounted the tops of their ladders and charge with the bayonet if any of them succeeded in getting over the stockade.

Some of the militiamen, on Caldwell's instructions, hurried into the nearby houses so that, from the upper windows, they could fire both at the barricade and over it into the men crowded in the narrow street behind. Already, as part of the planned defense of the post, there was a cannon mounted on a platform, positioned so that it could fire over the stockade.

The Rebels charged, clambering up the ladders onto the barricade, and the fire from the defenders mowed them down. Again and again they attacked as musket shot and grape from the barking cannon raked the top of the log barrier.

It was obvious that against the murderous density of shot that Caldwell could concentrate on the summit of the barricade, no one could get over it alive. The Rebels' only course was to weaken the defense, holding it down with heavy fire while they stormed again. So they swarmed into the houses on either side of the Sault-au-Matelot and opened fire from the upper windows, concentrating their shooting from the cover of the stone walls on the cannon crew, who, on their platform, were well exposed.

As an assault tactic it succeeded. The gunners leaped from the platform to take cover. On Caldwell's orders another gun was set up farther back along the curving hill road. This gun was out of sight of the Rebel marksmen, but because of its high position, it could fire on the houses that were sheltering them. Solid shot began to drop through the roofs, smashing the floors and stone walls.

So far, because of the narrow area on which Caldwell could concentrate his musket fire, none of the Americans had yet gotten over the barricade; but at one moment they came close to it. They swung a ladder over onto the defenders' side of the stockade so that if they could only surmount the top, they could get down fast into the street. A burly French-Canadian rushed to the barricade—exposing himself to pointblank fire through the loopholes—and wrenched the ladder away.

Almost immediately the colonel was faced with new danger. The Rebels had entered a house on one side of the barricade. The doorway was in the Sault-au-Matelot, but some of the side windows overlooked Caldwell's main defense position. From there the attackers would be able to shoot down at close range on the fusiliers and militia in the street below them.

It was a critical moment. A Highland Emigrant officer named Major Nairne grabbed the captured ladder, placed it against the side of the house, and then leaped up it, followed by the others. They met the Rebels coming into the house and fought them back down the stairs. "I called out to Nairne in their hearing," Caldwell reported later, "that he should let me know when he heard firing on the other side"—from the big party, in other words, that Carleton had sent outside the city to attack the Rebels from the rear.

The Governor's design to trap the Americans in the Sault-au-Matelot worked exactly as he planned. His men swarmed through the barricade at the other end of the street and demanded surrender from the Rebels, now hemmed in from both sides.

The first prisoners—each with a label pinned to his hat reading "Liberty or Death"—were passed through the window and down the ladder from the house that Nairne had taken. Then Caldwell had the gate in the barricade opened for the remainder.

Daniel Morgan, who would later win fame at Saratoga and in the Carolina campaign, was now in command (Arnold had been wounded and carried from the town). Refusing angrily to hand his sword to the British, whom he hated, Morgan insisted on giving it to a priest in the crowd.

In all, 426 Rebels were taken prisoner. Among the bodies lying in the snow outside the blockhouse on the western side of the Lower Town was the corpse of the Rebel General Montgomery. Carleton, who was often magnanimous, gave orders that it should be buried with full military honors.

Carleton had held Quebec, but the city was still under siege and there could be no relief until the spring. On the other hand Arnold—now commanding from a hospital bed in St. Roche—could be reinforced so that he could mount another assault on the walls.

The Rebels allowed the opportunity to pass. Arnold made a few attempts to fire the town with red-hot shot from batteries set up across both the St. Lawrence and the St. Charles—and on one occasion his men sailed a flaming fire ship into the harbor—but none of these efforts was successful. A virulent epidemic of smallpox severely weakened the morale of his men as they endured the extreme cold of those early weeks of 1776.

For Carleton, every day that passed increased his hopes of saving Quebec. In London, as he knew, two armies were being assembled to sail for America to smash the rebellion: a main force of twenty-five thousand men to join the troops in Boston, now commanded by General William Howe, and a smaller expedition of nine thousand men destined for Canada, which, after the recovery of the province, would strike south by way of Lake Champlain and the Hudson.

However, Lord George Germain, the newly appointed secretary for the colonies, had been warned that the Quebec garrison had only enough food to last until May. Ahead of the main troop convoys he sent an advance squadron of three ships carrying two hundred British regulars, with orders to get through to Quebec as early as they could.

On the morning of April 12 the three vessels were hove to in the Atlantic at the edge of a ten-foot thick ice field, "to which," as Captain Charles Douglas, the commander of the squadron, reported from the fifty-gun H.M.S. *Isis*, "we saw no bounds towards the western part of our horizon."

To test the strength of the vast field that lay between his ships and Canada, he ordered canvas. The helmsman of the *Isis* headed straight for the ice at a speed of five knots. The bow of the ship struck the frozen wall. For a few minutes the ship checked, shuddering; then the ice split, cracking loudly, and the vessel began to plow a channel.

"Encouraged by this experiment," Douglas wrote to the Admiralty jauntily, "we thought it . . . an effort due to the gallant defenders of Quebec to make the attempt of pressing her through by force of sail."

It was a bold decision, but progress was slow—so slow that the troops could be drilled on the ice beside the vessels as they plowed a passage. Blizzards and adverse winds delayed them further. It was not until May 6 that the frigate *Surprise*, sailing ahead of the others in the St. Lawrence, came in sight of the gaunt towers of the besieged city.

Fluttering at the head of the flagstaff was a blue pennant over a Union Jack, and five guns roared out from the walls—the agreed signal that the town was still in British hands.

Until then, Carleton had resisted stubbornly any temptation to attack his besiegers. But now that he had two hundred more regulars and the knowledge that thousands of reinforcements were on their way, he switched his policy to the offensive. His troops marched out of the gates onto the Plains of Abraham "to see what those mighty boasters are about," as he reported scathingly to London. "They were found very busy in their preparations to retreat . . . the plains were soon cleared of those plunderers; all their artillery, military stores etc were abandoned. . . ." Carleton led the pursuit, advancing up the St. Lawrence to the town of Three Rivers, where he set up temporary headquarters until the first of the troop convoys arrived at the end of May.

Apart from one small clash, the British were virtually unopposed by a Rebel force that was demoralized, appallingly diseased with smallpox, and torn by conflict between its commanders. The Americans retreated to Lake Champlain in a confusion that was not too great to prevent them from setting fire to Chambly and St. Johns as they passed.

By June the British had regained control of Canada and—though they lost America—they were never to release it again until the province ceased to be a colony. ☆

POSTSCRIPTS TO HISTORY

THE P.O.W. ISSUE
The genial treatment accorded the German officers and crew of the *Kronprinzessin Cecilie* at the outset of World War I ("The Sway of the Grand Saloon," October, 1971) was not altogether unusual in American military annals. There are some of us today who remember how well German prisoners of war were treated in detention camps in this country during the 1940's. But nothing can quite match the gratitude expressed by a Spanish infantryman who was captured when the American Army won the battle for Cuba in the summer of 1898. On the eve of being returned home to Spain that August, Private Pedro Lopez de Castillo wrote the following letter:

Soldiers of the American Army:
We would not be fulfilling our duty as well-born men, in whose breasts there lives gratitude and courtesy, should we embark for our beloved Spain without sending to you our most cordial and sincere good wishes and farewell. We fought you with ardor, with all our strength, endeavoring to gain the victory, but without the slightest rancor or hate toward the American nation. We have been vanquished by you (so our generals and chiefs judged in signing the capitulation), but our surrender and the bloody battles preceding it have left in our souls no place for resentment against the men who fought us nobly and valiantly. You fought and acted in compliance with the same call of duty as we, for we all but represent the power of our respective States. You fought us as men, face to face, and with great courage, as before stated, a quality which we had not met with during the three years we have carried on this war against a people without religion, without morals, without conscience, and of doubtful origin, who could not confront the enemy, but, hidden, spot their noble victims from ambush and then immediately fled. This was the kind of warfare we had to sustain in this unfortunate land. You have complied exactly with all the laws and usages of war as recognized by the armies of the most civilized nations of the world, have given honorable burial to the dead of the vanquished, have cured their wounded with great humanity, have respected and cared for your prisoners and their comfort, and, lastly, to us whose condition was terrible, you have given freely of food, of your stock of medicines, and you have honored us with distinction and courtesy, for after the fighting the two armies mingled with the utmost harmony. With this high sentiment of appreciation from us all, there remains but to express our farewell, and with the greatest sincerity we wish you all happiness and health in this land which will no longer belong to our dear Spain, but will be yours, who have conquered it by force and watered it with your blood, as your conscience called for, under the demand of civilization and humanity, but the descendants of the Congo and of Guinea, mingled with the blood of unscrupulous Spaniards and of traitors and adventurers, these people are not able to exercise or enjoy their liberty, for they will find it a burden to comply with the laws which govern civilized communities.
From 11,000 Spanish soldiers.

It is not likely that a similar letter, from a prisoner of either side, will be written after the Vietnam war is finally ended.

HISTORIANS AT ODDS
In our October, 1971, issue we printed part of a letter from Thomas J. Fleming, author of a history of West Point, criticizing "A Black Cadet at West Point" (August, 1971), by John F. Marszalek, Jr., for "a severe lack of historical perspective." Not surprisingly, Mr. Marszalek has reacted with equal vehemence. "Mr. Fleming's criticisms," he writes, "while presented with spirit and flourish, are not valid.... his knowledge of the entire matter, judging by his book's bibliography, was based mainly on a contemporary article written by a West Point professor before the court martial had met. As for the reversal of the decision, it came at a time when the nation had tired of the case and [it] won or lost few votes for the Arthur administration.... Mr. Fleming's insistence that the cadets would not have been stupid enough to make such a blunder as tying Whittaker, etc., is supposition and nothing more. It is just as logical to offer the supposition that Whittaker was not stupid either. Facts not suppositions determine truth...."

Rather than extending this interesting controversy any further, we suggest that concerned readers compare the article by Mr. Marszalek with the account of the Johnson Whittaker case given in Mr. Fleming's book, *West Point: The Men and Times of the United States Military Academy* (1969).

CONTEST WINNERS
In our issue of August, 1971, we offered to send complimentary copies of our extra issue *The Nineties* to readers who cited the most striking example of real persons named after

places, things, or events. We got a lot of entries, most of them documented, and many with an entertaining anecdote about the individual cited. The following names, which are accompanied by the names of those who submitted them, struck us as prize winners:

THROUGH TRIAL AND TRIBULATION WE ENTER INTO THE KINGDOM OF HEAVEN LINDLOFF. (Mrs. Robin Lodewick, Eugene, Oregon) The lad, who was born about 1900, was happily known as Trib.

States Rights Gist

STATES RIGHTS GIST. The name of this Confederate brigadier general was submitted by several readers, the first of whom was A. B. Hobbes, of Southbridge, Massachusetts. A South Carolinian, Gist fought in several important Civil War battles, including Vicksburg and Chickamauga. He was killed at Franklin, Tennessee, on the last day of November, 1864, while leading his brigade on foot after his horse had been shot. Caldwell Withers, of Columbia, South Carolina, who also sent in Gist's name, provided, in addition, the names of FORT SUMTER EARLE, who was mayor of Columbia from 1900 to 1904, and LAKE ERIE HIGH, a current resident of that city. And Hugh M. Thomason of Bowling Green, Kentucky, came up with the name of a colonel now in the Marine Corps, STATES RIGHTS JONES, JR.

BOSTON RASPBERRY. (John L. Roberts, Bonifay, Florida) Raspberry had been sentenced to life imprisonment for killing a rival player with a bat following a heated argument in a sand-lot baseball game. According to Mr. Roberts, Governor Millard Caldwell of Florida pardoned Raspberry, saying that "anybody with a name like 'Boston Raspberry' should have a full pardon."

CARBON PETROLEUM DUBBS. (The Reverend Paul C. Baker, Paris, Illinois)

SOUTH SIOUX BICKLEY. (A. James McArthur, Lincoln, Nebraska)

EASTER LILY GATES. (Mrs. Dorothy H. Wilken, University Park, Florida)

LAKE IHRIE. (Mrs. Jean Mitchell Green, Langhorne, Pennsylvania, Mr. Ihrie's granddaughter)

MORDECAI PETER CENTENNIAL BROWN. (Alan Fox, East Lansing, Michigan) "Three Finger" Brown, as he was known during his days as a major-league pitcher, was born in Indiana in 1876. He compiled an impressive record, pitching in 481 regular-season games and in nine World Series contests as a Chicago Cub between 1906 and 1910; he was elected to the Baseball Hall of Fame in 1949.

"Three Finger" Brown

EIFFEL TOWER SUTHERLAND. (Mrs. Helen Clark, Canton, Illinois, who also submitted DEW DAILY, UNIVERSITY OF TEXAS MITCHELL, and MERRY CHRISTMAS)

GOLD REFINED WILSON. (Milton Sernett, North East, Maryland)

BUDWEISER, FALSTAFF, and MICHELOB HAWKINS. (Mrs. Mary Francis Leisk, Las Vegas, Nevada)

E. PLURIBUS EUBANKS. (Frank Lang, Oakland, California)

OF BIRDS AND BEES

A number of the editors of this magazine happen to be graduates of Phillips Academy, the venerable preparatory school commonly known as Andover. One of them, going through a collection of Andover reminiscences recently, came upon the following brief memoir from the pen of Benjamin Spock, Andover '21, who later became famous as the author of a book on the raising of children that millions of parents have consulted as fervently as our ancestors did the Bible. Since Dr. Spock is known for his relaxed and liberal views about sexual education, among other things, we think "Andover and the Facts of Life" is a somewhat surprising as well as charming glimpse of the way things used to be.

Andover to me at sixteen was a revelation of worldliness. I had grown up in New Haven in an atmosphere that was certainly sheltered. The only dances I had attended were small 8-to-11 P.M. affairs in the homes of professional friends of my family. Someone's parent would drive us, and among those in the car would be one or two of my sisters. All of us at the party would be what the fussiest parent would call wholesome. I had gone to a small country day school with other boys equally protected. I remember that the picture, in Breasted's Short Ancient History, of the statue of the she-wolf suckling Romulus and Remus seemed risqué to us and caused the master to blush crimson.

Andover opened up new vistas. It's not that I did or saw anything wicked. But I listened attentively to all I heard, and

COPYRIGHT © 1959 BY PHILLIPS ACADEMY

dreamed of being a gay dog myself in Chicago or New York. The talk of friends about taking girls on individual dates was eyeopening. It seemed inconceivable to me that such freedom was permitted anywhere. A bit of gossip that made quite an impression was that, over Christmas vacation, one of our own classmates claimed to have been kissing an older woman of twenty-seven. That actual romances existed seemed proved by the arrival each day of tinted, scented letters, addressed to other occupants of the dormitory, in fancy girlish backhands. After I had been in school a few months, I couldn't stand it any longer. I bought a box of fine stationery with the seal of the school heavily embossed, and composed a fairly ardent letter to a girl at home. It must have surprised her because I had given her no earlier hint of such feelings.

Two classical courses gave me glimpses of the outside world. In Professor Forbes' class in Vergil I read that Aeneas had had an affair with Queen Dido in a cave, in which they had taken refuge during a thunder storm. It was surprising to me that a hero and a queen could forget their standards on such short acquaintance, and that this could be admitted in a text used in school. And one day in Greek, Professor Benner suddenly departed from his lecture and gave us a desperate-sounding plea to beware the faithlessness of women. It came so unexpectedly and was so obviously personal that it awed us into a goose fleshy attention. Looking back at this warning, I believe it increased rather than inhibited my interest in girls.

I did some outside reading. I found "Moll Flanders" in the school library through a pal's tip, and also had a brief chance to read passages from a book called, I think, "Confessions of a Bride," not from the library, which was being circulated privately at a rapid rate because of the urgency of the demand. I heard my first smutty stories. They made such an impression that I've never forgotten them, though I've had little success in remembering all the hundreds of funnier ones I've heard since. I had my first taste of liquor. An alumnus returning for the Exeter game had been billeted in our study. Since we hadn't invited him, we felt justified in taking an educational nip from a bottle of whiskey which he left in an open suitcase while he was reuning at his fraternity. The drop which I swallowed caused such an unexpected burning and choking that I was astounded to realize that this was the stuff so famed in song and story.

On a Sunday afternoon in the spring of senior year I was invited to come along with several friends who were going to call on an Andover family that included a couple of girls our age. Though the family was quite respectable, I sensed from the gaiety of my friends that they were not going because they were homesick for a touch of family life, and that the girls would probably not be quite as stand-offish as the ones I knew in New Haven. We sat around and we danced a little to the phonograph, nothing out of line. Yet there seemed—to me at least— an undertone of expectancy. Later I found myself in the pantry with one of the girls, getting pop and glasses for the crowd. I felt fairly sure that some approach from me would not make her indignant and that this was the moment to begin to be a roué. I felt dizzy while I hesitated. But soon the tray was ready and I had failed to come to any action. It was bitterly disappointing to realize that I had not become the gay dog I thought I had.

A mutton-chopped U. S. Grant
CHICAGO HISTORICAL SOCIETY

A still-life Dolley Madison
MAINE HISTORICAL SOCIETY

RARE PORTRAITS

Two rather unusual photographs have come into our hands. One is a profile of Ulysses S. Grant taken on June 2, 1875, when he occupied the White House. The photograph, which was called to our attention by Charles H. Branch of Memphis, Tennessee, shows the President without a beard or mustache, though still sporting mutton chops. According to one story, Grant's wife requested that he shave off his beard and mustache so that his likeness could be cut on a cameo. Another story has it that Grant had divested himself of his ornamentation at the request of the Treasury Department, which wanted to use his picture on paper currency; this currency, however, was never issued. The photograph was taken when Grant was fifty-three years old.

The other photograph is of Dolley Madison, and its rarity lies in the clearness of her visage. The wife of the nation's fourth President had an unfortunate habit of moving when her picture was taken, and other daguerreotypes of her always show her face blurred. The one reproduced here was brought to our attention by James B. Vickery of Brewer, Maine, who writes that the portrait was turned over to the Maine Historical Society in Portland in 1917 by Miss Mary G. Ray, "a daughter of Mrs. Joshua Wingate, who gave Dolley Madison the shawl she is wearing."

THE REVISIONIST: *The Cherry-Tree Caper, ca. 1740*

> FATHER, I CANNOT TELL A LIE. I HAVE TRASHED THE CHERRY TREE AS A PROTEST AGAINST THE ANTI-PROGRESSIVE, ANTI-ENVIRONMENTAL ATTITUDES OF THIS PLANTATION.

DRAWN BY MICHAEL RAMUS